AF706061

Adam Raźniewski

From Prototype to Product

Building Commercial Devices with Raspberry Pi

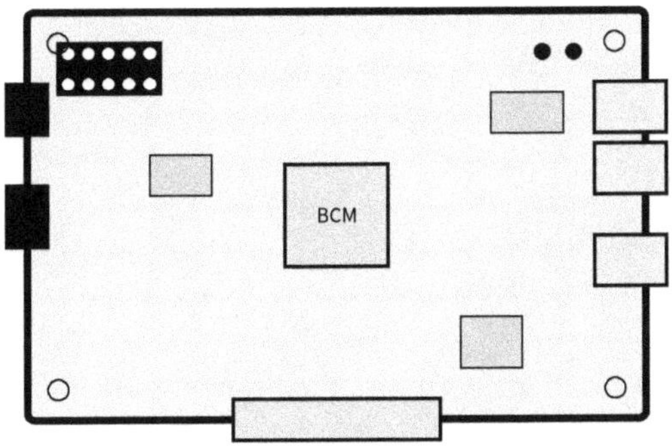

Raz Publish

Adam Raźniewski

From Prototype to Product

Building Commercial Devices with Raspberry Pi

Raz Publish

Edition 1, 2025

Copyright © 2025 Adam Raźniewski

All rights reserved. No part of this publication may be reproduced, distributed, or transmitted in any form or by any means, including photocopying, recording, or other electronic or mechanical methods, without the prior written permission of the author, except in the case of brief quotations embodied in critical reviews and certain other noncommercial uses permitted by copyright law.

For permission requests, contact the author at https://razniewski.eu

This book is provided "as is"without warranty of any kind, express or implied. The author shall not be liable for any damages arising from the use of this information.

This publication is available in the following editions:

- Hardcover — ISBN 978-83-977396-2-8
- Paperback — ISBN 978-83-977396-1-1
- eBook — ISBN 978-83-977396-0-4

Published by Raz Publish

Preambule

I HAVE SPENT YEARS BUILDING devices based on Raspberry Pi: time attendance machines, camera boards, thermal vision systems, access control devices, even a self-service beer tap (Cybertap).

For a long time, I wished there was a book like this one. A book that didn't just show the theory, but told the truth about what it really takes to move from an idea to a production-ready product.

I made plenty of mistakes along the way. I chose the wrong boards, I burned Raspberry Pis, I lost months fixing devices. At one point, I was spending eight hours a day repairing customer units because my devices would only last one year — while I was offering a two-year warranty. The biggest lesson? Never rely on SD cards in production.

Despite the failures, I kept going. Over time, I sold more than 5000 of my devices worldwide. Every project taught me something new, and those lessons are what I want to share with you here.

If you want to create devices, put them into the market, and avoid the mistakes I made — this book is for you.

About Author

I'm Adam, and I love to create, program, and build. I've always been curious about technology and people, and I enjoy not only designing but also selling what I create.

My first company was born while I was still at university—StudentsCode. Back then, I ran Minecraft servers that surprisingly brought me both a good income and my future wife. Later, I worked at Siemens as a Software Architect, and then at the Texas startup Codenotary, where I grew from Software Developer to Chief Architect over the course of three years.

Eventually, I returned to what had always been close to me: Raspberry Pi. I began producing my own devices, learning the hard way what it means to build for real customers and ship hardware worldwide.

Today, I have designed and delivered thousands of devices based on Raspberry Pi technology, ranging from time attendance systems to access control units, thermal vision cameras, and self-service beer machines. This book collects the lessons I've learned along that journey.

Table of Contents

1
Analyzing the Problem

Before writing a single line of code or ordering any components, you must crystallize exactly what problem you're solving. This chapter presents a systematic framework for transforming vague business requirements into concrete technical architecture.

Most hardware projects fail not because of technical limitations, but because the problem was never properly defined. I've seen teams spend months building elegant solutions to the wrong problem, only to discover their fundamental assumptions were flawed.

1.1 The Problem Definition Framework

Every successful device project starts with answering one fundamental question: **What do I want to build?**

This seems obvious, but most initial problem statements are too vague for implementation. "I want to build a time attendance system"tells you nothing about authentication methods, data storage, network requirements, or user interface needs.

1.1.1 Step 1: Core Function Definition

Start with a single sentence that captures the essential transformation your device performs:

> Example: Time Attendance Registrator
>
> **Core Function:** Upon user authentication, the device records an attendance event with timestamp and user identity.

> Example: Self-Service Beer Machine
>
> **Core Function:** Authenticate user, calculate beer price, process payment, dispense measured amount of beer, and display product information.

> Example: Smart Helmet
>
> **Core Function:** Stream real-time video and thermal imaging from field operations to command center while maintaining authentication and local storage backup.

1.1.2 Step 2: Core Function Problem Solve Proposal

Once you've defined what your device does, determine how it will accomplish that core function. This step identifies the primary technical challenge and your proposed solution approach.

For each core function, ask: What is the most critical technical problem I need to solve?

Time Attendance Registrator:

- **Primary Challenge:** Reliably identifying users without manual input
- **Solution Proposal:** RFID-based authentication with local database storage
- **Why:** 99% success rate (1% is when employees share the card), low cost, works offline, minimal user training

Self-Service Beer Machine:

- **Primary Challenge:** Accurate volume measurement for variable pricing
- **Solution Proposal:** Flow sensor with real-time price calculation
- **Why:** Enables user-controlled portions while maintaining precise billing

Smart Helmet:

- **Primary Challenge:** Real-time video transmission with network reliability issues
- **Solution Proposal:** Local buffering with automatic upload when connectivity restored
- **Why:** Ensures no data loss during network outages in mission-critical applications

1.1.3 Step 3: Authentication Requirements Analysis

Authentication patterns vary significantly across device types. Identify which pattern fits your project:

Type 1: Local User Authentication (Time Attendance) User authenticates locally for service access, administrator authenticates remotely for reports and management.

Type 2: Cloud-Connected User Authentication (Cybertap) User authenticates locally, but device must communicate with cloud to validate account balance and process transactions.

Type 3: Device-to-Cloud Authentication (Smart Helmet) No user authentication - the helmet itself authenticates to cloud services using unique API key for secure communication.

Time Attendance Registrator - Authentication Options:

Method	Success Rate	Cost	Complexity
RFID Card	99%	Low	Low
QR Code Scan	95%	Low	Medium
Barcode Scan	98%	Low	Medium
Bluetooth Phone ID	85%	Medium	High
Fingerprint	90%	High	High
Face Recognition	85%	High	Very High

Tabela 1.1: Authentication method comparison

Key insight: RFID provides the best balance of reliability, cost, and implementation simplicity. Biometric options sound sophisticated but introduce significant complexity for marginal business value.

1.1.4 Step 4: Interface Requirements

List all required interfaces before considering implementation:

Time Attendance System Interfaces:

- **User Authentication Interface:** RFID reader, status LEDs, audio feedback
- **Administrative Interface:** Web-based user management, report generation

- **Network Interface:** Remote access for data export and system configuration
- **Data Interface:** Local storage with cloud synchronization capability

Self-Service Beer Machine Interfaces:

- **User Interface:** Card reader, balance display, dispense button, volume display
- **Product Interface:** Flow measurement sensor, flow control valve, temperature monitoring
- **Device Interface:** Product identification (each device = one beer type), price per ml configuration
- **Network Interface:** Card balance synchronization, transaction logging, device status reporting

Smart Helmet Interfaces:

- **Video Interface:** 4K camera, thermal imaging sensor, real-time streaming
- **Communication Interface:** Command center authentication, network failover handling
- **Storage Interface:** Local video buffering, automatic upload when connectivity restored
- **Power Interface:** Battery management, charging protocols, power-saving modes

1.2 System Architecture Mapping

Once interfaces are defined, create a system block diagram showing data and control flows.

1.2.1 Time Attendance System Architecture

Required Functions:

- **User identification function:** Read unique identifier from user credential
- **Data processing function:** Match identifier to user database, record timestamp
- **User feedback function:** Indicate successful/failed authentication to user
- **Data storage function:** Store attendance records locally with backup capability
- **Communication function:** Sync data and receive configuration updates
- **Administrative function:** Manage users and generate reports remotely

Critical architectural decisions:

- Local database required for offline operation
- Network interface must handle intermittent connectivity
- Status feedback essential for user confidence
- Administrative interface needed for user management

1.2.2 Self-Service Beer Machine Architecture

Required Functions:

- **Authentication function:** Read and validate user card credentials

- **Balance management function:** Check available balance, deduct costs locally
- **Flow control function:** Start/stop beer dispensing based on user control
- **Measurement function:** Accurately measure dispensed volume for pricing
- **Display function:** Show current balance, volume dispensed, and cost
- **Synchronization function:** Update card balances and transaction logs with central system

Critical architectural decisions:

- Local card balance caching required for offline operation
- Each device represents one beer type (no product selection needed)
- Flow measurement essential for accurate pricing per ml
- Network synchronization needed for card balance updates
- Simplified user interface (no payment terminal required)

1.2.3 Smart Helmet Architecture

Required Functions:

- **Video capture function:** Record high-resolution visible light video
- **Thermal imaging function:** Capture and process thermal camera data

- **Authentication function:** Identify helmet to command center systems
- **Streaming function:** Transmit real-time video feeds with low latency
- **Storage function:** Buffer video locally during network outages
- **Power management function:** Monitor battery, optimize power consumption
- **Communication function:** Handle multiple network types with automatic failover

Critical architectural decisions:

- Video encoding must happen locally to reduce bandwidth requirements
- Local storage essential for network outage scenarios
- Battery monitoring critical for field operation safety
- Dual camera streams require significant processing power
- Multiple network interfaces needed for mission-critical reliability

1.3 Constraint Analysis

Every project has hidden constraints that aren't obvious from the initial requirements. Identify these early:

1.3.1 Physical Constraints

- **Mounting requirements:** Time attendance device must be wall-mountable with standard hardware
- **Chemical resistance:** Beer machine components must resist beer acid and cleaning chemicals
- **Size limitations:** Smart helmet PCB must be compact enough to integrate into helmet design
- **Environmental conditions:** Operating temperature, humidity, vibration resistance
- **Power requirements:** Battery life, charging infrastructure, power consumption limits

1.3.2 Performance Constraints

- **Response time:** Attendance registration under 0.3 seconds (nobody likes to wait), beer dispense start under 2 seconds (somehow people likes beer more that time attendance :))
- **Accuracy requirements:** Payment processing 100% accurate, video quality standards
- **Reliability targets:** 99.9% uptime, mean time between failures
- **Capacity limits:** Concurrent users, data storage requirements, network bandwidth

1.3.3 Business Constraints

- **Cost targets:** Manufacturing cost per unit, development budget limits

- **Time constraints:** Market window, certification timelines
- **Regulatory requirements:** Payment card compliance, safety certifications
- **Support requirements:** Field serviceability, remote diagnostics capability

1.4 Common Analysis Mistakes

Avoid these frequent errors that lead to project failure:

> **Warning: Feature Creep**
>
> Resist the temptation to add "nice to have"features during analysis. Every additional feature exponentially increases complexity, cost, and failure probability. Focus ruthlessly on core requirements.

Other critical mistakes:

- **Underestimating power requirements:** Always measure actual power consumption, don't trust datasheets
- **Ignoring certification requirements:** FCC, CE, safety certifications can add months to timeline
- **Assuming perfect network connectivity:** Design for intermittent and unreliable networks
- **Overlooking field serviceability:** Plan for diagnostics, updates, and repairs from day one

1.5 Moving to Implementation

The next step is translating this analysis into electronic interfaces and component selection. But first, validate your analysis with potential customers.

Show them your interface requirements. Their feedback at this stage costs nothing to incorporate. Changes after you've ordered components cost everything.

Remember: hours spent in problem analysis save weeks in implementation and months in field debugging. The most expensive mistake is building the right solution to the wrong problem.

2
Vision into Electronic Interfaces

TRANSLATING FUNCTIONAL REQUIREMENTS into specific electronic components is where most hardware projects either succeed or fail spectacularly. This chapter walks through the systematic process of selecting components, using a time attendance system as our example.

The key is methodical evaluation: never choose the first component you find, and never assume compatibility without verification.

2.1 Component Selection Process

Let's build a time attendance system step by step, making real component choices with real tradeoffs.

2.1.1 Step 1: Identify Core Components

From our problem analysis, we need:

- RFID reader for user identification
- Processing unit for database operations
- Network interface for data synchronization
- Local storage (non-volatile)
- User feedback system

2.1.2 Step 2: RFID Reader Selection

Starting with RFID, I search development boards compatible with Raspberry Pi. Two modules dominate the market:

RC522 RFID Module - €3 from Botland (https://botland.store/rfid-modules-tags/6765-rfid-mf-rc522-module-1356mhz-spi-card-and-keychain-5904422335014.html)

PN532 RFID Module - €12-15 from various suppliers

Component comparison:

Specification	RC522	PN532
Price	€3	€12-15
Library Support (RPi)	Excellent	Limited maintenance
Communication	SPI	I2C/SPI/UART
NFC Support	No	Yes
Range	Standard	Slightly better

Tabela 2.1: RFID module comparison

Critical evaluation questions:

RC522 Analysis:

- **Is this chip widely manufactured?** Yes - RC522 is produced by multiple manufacturers
- **Is it obsolete or current?** The chip is older but still in active production

- **Library support available?** Multiple libraries exist, including my fork for CM4/CM5 kernels (https://github.com/Razikus/razrc522)
- **Cost vs. alternatives?** €3 is competitive for 13.56MHz RFID

PN532 Analysis:

- **Additional capabilities:** NFC support, multiple communication interfaces
- **Library maintenance:** Raspberry Pi libraries are poorly maintained, often outdated
- **Cost impact:** 4-5x more expensive than RC522
- **Production risk:** Limited library support increases development and maintenance burden

Decision: RC522 selected. For time attendance, NFC capability provides no additional value. RC522's lower cost and established library ecosystem outweigh PN532's theoretical advantages.

2.1.3 Step 3: Processing Unit Selection

For Raspberry Pi-based systems, the choice is between standard Pi boards and Compute Modules.

My rule: Never use SD cards in production devices. Period.

This eliminates standard Raspberry Pi boards and directs us to Compute Modules with eMMC storage.

Compute Module 4 - Example: CM4102008

- 2GB RAM, 8GB eMMC, WiFi
- Price: €85 from Farnell
- **Why 2GB RAM?** 1GB is insufficient for modern applications

- **Why 8GB eMMC?** Adequate for OS + application + local database
- **Why not CM5?** Excessive processing power, higher heat generation, unnecessary cost

Critical insight: CM5 lacks hardware H.264 encoding - video applications will consume significant CPU resources for encoding tasks.

2.1.4 Step 4: Carrier Board Decision

Two paths for CM4 integration:

Option 1: Development Carrier Board Waveshare CM4-IO-BASE-C provides cameras, GPIO access, standard interfaces.

Advantages:

- Immediate availability
- No custom PCB design required
- Good for prototyping and small quantities

Disadvantages:

- Requires manual cable assembly
- Not optimized for production assembly
- Higher per-unit cost at scale

Option 2: Custom Production Board Purpose-built carrier with dedicated connectors (example: https://shop.razniewski.eu/p/cm4pb)

Advantages:

- Optimized for production assembly

- TE connectors for RC522, buzzer, indicators
- Lower assembly cost per unit
- Professional appearance

Disadvantages:

- Requires PCB design and tooling investment
- Minimum order quantities
- Longer development timeline

Production volume decision threshold: Above 100 units, custom boards become cost-effective.

2.2 Component Replaceability Strategy

> **Critical Lesson: Component Obsolescence**
>
> We ordered 1000 units after selling our first 100. The Ethernet connector went end-of-life between orders. Fortunately, a replacement existed, but required minor case modifications. Had we used a proprietary micro-USB connector, we would have faced complete redesign.

Replaceability guidelines:

- Choose standard form factors (USB-A, RJ45, standard pin headers)
- Avoid proprietary connectors unless absolutely necessary
- Design footprints that accommodate multiple manufacturer variants
- Document acceptable part substitutions in BOM

2.3 Connector and Cable Strategy

For production devices, cable assemblies determine assembly time and reliability.

Custom Cable Manufacturing: LCSC (https://www.lcsc.com/customcables) provides professional cable assemblies with proper strain relief and connectors.

Example connector choice: TE 3-640621-8 (8-pin connector) - Standard series with multiple variants - Available from multiple suppliers - Established assembly processes

Production assembly goal: Connect RC522 module, connect I/O board, install in case, ship. Minimize field wiring and soldering.

2.4 Camera Integration Considerations

Camera selection depends on processing requirements and driver availability.

USB Cameras with V4L2 Support

- Easiest integration path
- Standard Linux drivers
- No custom kernel modifications required

CSI Cameras

- Higher performance potential
- Requires Raspberry Pi-specific drivers
- CM4 hardware acceleration available

Real Example: Kopin A914 Integration

SmartHelmet project required Kopin A914 microdisplay integration via MIPI-DSI. Custom kernel driver development became necessary. The process was challenging enough with standard Linux development - on Balena platform, documentation was nonexistent, requiring extensive trial-and-error with similar drivers.

Camera selection priority:

1. Standard USB with V4L2 support
2. CSI with established Raspberry Pi drivers
3. Custom hardware only when absolutely necessary

2.5 Microcontroller vs. Raspberry Pi Decision

Not every project requires Raspberry Pi processing power.

Use ESP32 when:

- Simple data collection and transmission
- Low power requirements critical
- Cost optimization paramount
- Real-time response requirements

Use Raspberry Pi when:

- Edge processing required
- Complex user interfaces needed
- Local database operations

- Video/audio processing
- Standard Linux software stack beneficial

Time attendance system evaluation: Requires local database, web interface, and network synchronization. Raspberry Pi appropriate choice.

2.6 Power and Performance Considerations

CM4 vs. CM5 comparison for production:

Specification	CM4	CM5
Processing Power	Adequate for most apps	Excessive for many cases
Heat Generation	Manageable	Requires active cooling
Hardware H.264 Encoding	Yes	No (CPU-based)
Power Consumption	Lower	Higher
Cost	Lower	Higher

Tabela 2.2: CM4 vs CM5 production comparison

Recommendation: CM4 remains optimal for most production applications unless specific CM5 features are required.

2.7 Validation and Testing Strategy

Before committing to large quantities:

1. **Prototype with development boards:** Verify functionality with Waveshare or similar carrier boards

2. **Test component availability:** Order small quantities from multiple suppliers
3. **Validate software libraries:** Ensure drivers work with your kernel version
4. **Thermal testing:** Verify thermal performance in your enclosure
5. **Production assembly test:** Build 5-10 units with production processes

2.8 Documentation for Production

Create these documents before scaling:

- **Bill of Materials (BOM):** Include acceptable substitutions
- **Assembly instructions:** Step-by-step with photos
- **Test procedures:** Functional verification steps
- **Connector pinouts:** Cable assembly documentation
- **Software configuration:** Deployment and setup procedures

2.9 Moving Forward

With components selected and interfaces defined, the next step is building the "spider prototype- a functional system using development boards and jumper wires to validate the complete system integration before committing to custom PCB design.

Remember: the goal is not perfect component selection, but systematic evaluation that minimizes risk while maintaining cost targets. Every component choice creates dependencies - choose components that provide multiple supply sources and established ecosystem support.

3

Build a "spider"prototype

You've analyzed the problem and selected components. Now comes the critical validation phase: proving your concept actually works before committing to PCB design and production tooling.

This is the transition from TRL 3 (experimental proof of concept) to TRL 4 (technology validated in lab). The "spider"prototype gets its name from the web of jumper wires connecting components - it looks chaotic but serves a crucial purpose.

3.1 The Technology Readiness Level Context

Understanding where you are in the development process prevents premature optimization:

TRL 1-2: Basic principles and concept formulation (completed in analysis phase) **TRL 3:** Experimental proof of concept (what we're building now) **TRL 4:** Technology validated in lab environment (our goal for this chapter) **TRL 5-6:** Validation in relevant/operational environment (future chapters) **TRL 7-9:** System demonstration and proven operation (production phase)

3.2 Spider Prototype Objectives

The spider prototype must validate every critical function:

For our time attendance system:

- RFID reader successfully captures UID
- CM4 maintains stable internet connection
- System executes REST API calls reliably
- Buzzer provides audio feedback
- GPIO controls function correctly
- Data persistence works (file or database)
- Web interface displays collected data

3.3 Minimal Software Requirements

Write the simplest possible code that exercises every function:

Basic Validation Script

```
import time
import requests
from razrc522.rfid import RFID
from razrc522.easyrfid import EasyRFID, EasyRFIDUIDMode, EasyRFIDAuth
reader = RFID(antenna_gain=7, logger=None)
easyRFID = EasyRFID(reader, mode=EasyRFIDUIDMode.HEX)
def test_network():
    try:
        response = requests.get('https://httpbin.org/get', timeout=5)
        return response.status_code == 200
    except:
        return False
def read_rfid_card():
    try:
        convertedUID, rawUID = easyRFID.wait_and_select()
        block = 0
        # Standard MIFARE 1k key
        authorized = easyRFID.authorize(EasyRFIDAuth.AuthB,
                                        [0xFF, 0xFF, 0xFF, 0xFF, 0xFF, 0xFF],
                                        rawUID, block)
        if authorized:
            readed = easyRFID.read_block(block)
            ....
...
```

3.4 Critical Validation Questions

Run your spider prototype and systematically evaluate:

3.4.1 Basic Functionality

- **Does it work at all?** Can you complete the full cycle without errors?
- **How cumbersome is interaction?** Does RFID reading require multiple attempts?
- **Response time:** How fast does the system respond to card presentation?
- **Reliability:** Test the same operation 50 times - how many succeed?

3.4.2 Environmental Factors

- **Heat generation:** Does the CM4 require cooling under normal operation?
- **Power consumption:** Measure actual current draw vs. specifications
- **Voltage compatibility:** Verify 3.3V GPIO levels work with your peripherals
- **EMI sensitivity:** Do nearby phones or WiFi networks cause interference?

3.4.3 Persistence Testing

- **24-hour test:** Does the system work reliably after running overnight?

- **1-hour stress test:** Continuous operation with frequent card reads
- **Network interruption:** How does the system behave when WiFi disconnects?
- **Power cycle recovery:** Does it restart cleanly after power loss?

> **Critical Voltage Warning**
>
> Raspberry Pi GPIO operates at 3.3V, not 5V. Connecting 5V signals to GPIO pins will damage your CM4. Always verify peripheral voltage requirements and use level shifters when necessary.

3.5 Spider Prototype Assembly

Option 1: Individual Components
Required components for time attendance validation:

- CM4 on development carrier board (Waveshare CM4-IO-BASE-C or similar)
- RC522 RFID module
- Buzzer (3.3V compatible)
- LED for status indication
- Breadboard and jumper wires
- RFID cards/tags for testing

Connection diagram:

```
RC522 -> CM4 GPIO
SDA   -> GPIO 8  (SPI CE0)
SCK   -> GPIO 11 (SPI CLK)
MOSI  -> GPIO 10 (SPI MOSI)
MISO  -> GPIO 9  (SPI MISO)
RST   -> GPIO 25
3.3V  -> 3.3V
GND   -> GND

Buzzer -> GPIO 18
LED    -> GPIO 24 (with resistor)
```

Option 2: Complete RFID Solution

For faster prototyping, use the complete CM4 RFID board (https://shop.razniewski.eu/p/cm4pb) which includes CM4, RFID reader, and all necessary interfaces pre-integrated. This eliminates wiring complexity and reduces validation time to software testing only.

3.6 Iteration and Refinement

Spider prototypes exist to fail safely. Expect multiple iterations:

Common first iteration failures:

- RFID reading inconsistent (adjust antenna positioning)
- Network timeouts (implement retry logic)
- GPIO conflicts (verify pin assignments)
- Power supply inadequate (check current requirements)

Performance optimization targets:

- RFID read success rate > 95%

- Response time < 2 seconds
- Network operation timeout < 5 seconds
- System uptime > 24 hours without intervention

Material interference testing: Test RFID scanning through different materials, particularly those you plan to use for the final enclosure:

- Plastic enclosure materials (ABS, polycarbonate)
- Metal proximity effects (mounting screws, brackets)
- Glass or acrylic cover materials
- Varying material thicknesses

3.7 Component Validation Results

After spider prototype testing, you'll know definitively:

Keep these components if:

- Functionality works reliably in spider configuration
- Performance meets your requirements
- Heat generation is manageable
- Cost targets are achievable

Reconsider components if:

- Reliability issues persist after optimization attempts
- Performance significantly below expectations
- Integration complexity exceeds development budget
- Alternative components offer substantial advantages

3.8 Decision Point: PCB or Software First

With validated spider prototype, choose your next development path:

PCB Design First:

- Hardware functionality proven stable
- Mechanical constraints well understood
- Production timeline pressure
- External PCB design resources available

Software Development First:

- Complex software requirements
- User interface needs refinement
- Integration with external systems required
- Software team available in-house

My typical approach: Software development while PCB design proceeds in parallel. Software can be developed and tested on spider prototype while PCB layout is completed by external partners.

3.9 External PCB Design Considerations

Most hardware entrepreneurs benefit from partnering with PCB design specialists rather than learning complex layout tools.

First PCB reality check: Your first PCB will not be ready for final enclosure integration. Accept this from the start.

At this point, consider your enclosure strategy by reviewing the Appendix resources:

- **Kradex:** Standard enclosures for cost-effective solutions
- **Cubic Inch:** Custom 3D printed enclosures for unique requirements

Think about placement and constraints, but don't optimize yet:

- How will components be positioned relative to each other?
- What connectors need external access?
- Where will status indicators be visible?
- How will the RFID antenna be oriented?

Mechanical constraints will change as you iterate. The PCB will evolve significantly between first prototype and production version.

Prepare for external PCB design:

- Detailed pinout documentation from spider prototype
- Basic mechanical requirements (board size, connector positions)
- Performance requirements (signal integrity, EMI considerations)
- Manufacturing constraints (assembly capabilities, test points)

Iteration expectation: Plan for 2 PCB iterations minimum. The first validates electrical functionality. The second optimizes for mechanical integration and manufacturing.

3.10 Moving to Implementation

Your spider prototype has validated the core technology. You now have:

- Proven component functionality
- Working software foundation
- Performance baselines
- Integration challenges identified
- Development path clarity

The next phase involves either developing production software on your proven hardware platform or translating the spider prototype into a proper PCB design that maintains the validated functionality while enabling efficient manufacturing.

Remember: the spider prototype's job is to fail fast and fail cheap. Every failure discovered here saves weeks of debugging production hardware later.

4
Write a Software

Your POC works and hardware is validated. Now comes the transition from proof-of-concept scripts to production software that customers can rely on. This chapter covers the systematic approach to building robust embedded applications.

Production software differs fundamentally from development scripts. It must handle edge cases, recover from failures, and operate unattended for months. Every decision impacts long-term reliability and maintainability.

4.1 Network Management

4.1.1 NetworkManager and D-Bus Integration

Use NetworkManager via D-Bus for all network operations. This provides system-level integration and handles complex scenarios like WiFi roaming and connection management automatically.

Avoid: Direct manipulation of network interfaces or configuration files **Use:** NetworkManager D-Bus API for programmatic control

Hotspot Creation Example

```
#!/usr/bin/env python
# NetworkManager hotspot creation via D-Bus
import dbus, sys, time

our_uuid = "2b0d0f1d-b79d-43af-bde"
s_ip4 = dbus.Dictionary({"method": "shared"})
s_ip6 = dbus.Dictionary({"method": "ignore"})
con = dbus.Dictionary({
    "connection": s_con,
    "802-11-wireless": s_wifi,
    "802-11-wireless-security": s_wsec,
    "ipv4": s_ip4,
    "ipv6": s_ip6,
})
connection_path = None
for path in settings.ListConnections():
    proxy = bus.get_object("org.freedesktop.
   NetworkManager", path)
    settings_connection = dbus.Interface(
        proxy, "org.freedesktop.NetworkManager.
   Settings.Connection"
    )
    config = settings_connection.GetSettings()
    if config["connection"]["uuid"] == our_uuid
   :
        connection_path = path
        break
```

4.1.2 Service Management with systemd

Use systemd for service management rather than Docker unless containerization provides specific benefits. For embedded systems, systemd's overhead is minimal and integration is superior.

Systemd advantages for embedded systems:

- Native process supervision and restart
- Dependency management between services
- Resource limiting and monitoring
- Integration with system logging
- No container runtime overhead

4.1.3 Bluetooth Network Configuration

For Bluetooth network functionality, create NAP (Network Access Point) using bt-network:

Bluetooth NAP Setup

```
# Create Bluetooth network access point
bt-network NAP pan0

# Configure IP for pan0 interface
ip addr add 192.168.100.1/24 dev pan0
ip link set pan0 up

# Enable IP forwarding for internet sharing
echo 1 > /proc/sys/net/ipv4/ip_forward
iptables -A FORWARD -i pan0 -j ACCEPT
iptables -t nat -A POSTROUTING -o wlan0 -j
    MASQUERADE
```

4.2 System Reliability and Auto-Healing

4.2.1 Comprehensive Auto-Healing Strategy

Production devices must recover automatically from any recoverable failure. Implement multiple layers of monitoring and recovery.

The fundamental principle is simple: it's better for a service to restart than to crash and stay down. Your customers expect devices to work continuously without manual intervention. Every failure that requires human intervention scales poorly and damages your reputation.

A device that restarts gracefully when problems occur appears more reliable to customers than one that crashes and requires physical intervention. Plan for failure from the beginning.

Application-level monitoring:

Simple Watchdog Script

```
#!/bin/bash
check_service() {
    if ! systemctl is-active --quiet $1; then
        systemctl restart $1
        sleep 5
        systemctl is-active --quiet $1 || /sbin/reboot
    fi
}
while true; do
    check_service "time-attendance"
    check_service "hotspot-manager"
    sleep 30
done
```

4.2.2 Security Hardening

Close unnecessary services and ports. Embedded devices should expose minimal attack surface.

Essential hardening steps:

- Disable unused systemd services
- Configure iptables to block unused ports
- Remove or disable SSH after initial setup
- Use fail2ban for brute force protection
- Regular security updates via controlled update mechanism

4.3 Storage and Logging Strategy

4.3.1 Minimal Disk Logging

Critical principle: Minimize disk writes to extend storage life.

Unlike server applications, embedded systems must minimize storage wear. Use in-memory storage with periodic persistence.

Logging strategy:

- Use systemd journal with volatile storage (RAM-based)
- Log only critical events to persistent storage
- Implement log rotation with aggressive size limits
- Use ring buffers for debug information

Journal configuration for embedded systems:

/etc/systemd/journald.conf

```
[Journal]
Storage=none
RuntimeMaxUse=16M
RuntimeMaxFiles=5
MaxLevelStore=warning
MaxLevelSyslog=err
```

4.3.2 Efficient Data Storage with Redis

For application data storage, Redis provides excellent performance with configurable persistence.

Redis configuration for embedded systems:

Redis Persistence Configuration

```
# redis.conf - optimized for embedded systems

# Save every 100 keys changed OR every 60 seconds
save 60 1
save 300 100
save 900 1000

# Use less memory
maxmemory 64mb
maxmemory-policy allkeys-lru

# Disable AOF for minimal writes
appendonly no

# Optimize for low-power systems
hz 10
```

Application integration example:

Redis Usage Pattern

```
import redis
import json
import time

class AttendanceStorage:
    def __init__(self):
        self.redis = redis.Redis(host=’localhost’, port=6379, db=0)

    def log_attendance(self, user_id, timestamp=None):
        if timestamp is None:
            timestamp = int(time.time())

        # Store in Redis
        key = f"attendance:{timestamp}"
        data = {"user_id": user_id, "timestamp": timestamp}
        self.redis.setex(key, 86400, json.dumps(data))  # 24h TTL

        # Add to daily summary
        date_key = f"daily:{time.strftime(’%Y-%m-%d’, time.localtime(timestamp))}"
        self.redis.sadd(date_key, user_id)
        self.redis.expire(date_key, 86400 * 30)  # 30 day retention

    def get_daily_attendance(self, date):
        date_key = f"daily:{date}"
        return list(self.redis.smembers(date_key))
```

4.4 User Interface Development

4.4.1 Raylib for Embedded Graphics

For applications requiring local display, Raylib provides efficient graphics with minimal dependencies.

Raylib advantages for embedded systems:

- Small footprint and minimal dependencies
- Hardware-accelerated graphics where available
- Cross-platform compatibility
- Simple API for common UI elements
- Good performance on low-power hardware

Basic Raylib application structure:

Simple Attendance Display

```
#include "raylib.h"
#include <stdio.h>
int main(void) {
    const int screenWidth = 800;
    const int screenHeight = 480;
    InitWindow(screenWidth, screenHeight, "Attendance System");
    SetTargetFPS(30);
    char statusText[256] = "Ready for card...";
    int cardCount = 0;
    while (!WindowShouldClose()) {
        if (IsKeyPressed(KEY_SPACE)) {  // Simulate card scan
            cardCount++;
            sprintf(statusText, "Card scanned! Total: %d", cardCount);
        }
        BeginDrawing();
        ClearBackground(DARKBLUE);
        DrawText("Time Attendance System", 150, 50, 40, WHITE);
        DrawText(statusText, 200, 200, 20, YELLOW);
        DrawText("Press SPACE to simulate card scan", 200, 350, 16, GRAY);
        EndDrawing();
    }
    CloseWindow();
    return 0;
}
```

4.5 Remote Update Capability

4.5.1 Update System Requirements

Every production device must support remote updates. Design this capability from the beginning, not as an afterthought.

Update system components:

- Cryptographically signed update packages
- Rollback capability for failed updates
- Health check monitoring post-update
- Bandwidth-efficient delta updates
- Scheduled update windows to minimize disruption

4.6 Dependency Management and Backup Strategy

4.6.1 Critical Reality: Everything Becomes Obsolete

External dependencies disappear, break, or become incompatible. You must backup everything—not just Python packages, but the entire system.

What breaks without warning:

- APT packages removed from repositories
- Docker base images deleted or updated incompatibly
- GitHub repositories disappearing
- Kernel driver compatibility broken by updates

4.6.2 Full System Backup Approach

Complete system image: Create full disk images of working systems:

- `dd if=/dev/mmcblk0 of=working-v1.0.img`
- Store multiple dated snapshots
- Include bootloader and partition table
- Test restoration on clean hardware

Package cache backup:

APT Package Backup

```
# Backup all downloaded packages
cp -r /var/cache/apt/archives/ /backup/apt-cache/

# Backup package lists
dpkg --get-selections > /backup/packages.list

# Backup sources.list
cp /etc/apt/sources.list /backup/
```

Docker Reality Check

Docker images frequently become obsolete. Base images get updated, breaking your builds. Always backup working containers as .tar files and test restoration regularly. Don't trust Docker Hub to maintain old versions.

Offline rebuild capability: Verify you can rebuild everything without internet:

- Test package installation from local cache
- Verify all dependencies are archived
- Document exact build procedures
- Keep working system images as fallback

4.7 Support and Diagnostics

4.7.1 Built-in Diagnostic Capabilities

Production software must include comprehensive diagnostic tools for remote troubleshooting.

Essential diagnostic information:

- System health metrics (CPU, memory, temperature)
- Network connectivity status and performance
- Storage usage and health indicators
- Application-specific status (RFID reader, database)
- Recent error logs and event history

4.8 Additional Service Opportunities

4.8.1 SSL Proxy and Remote Access

Once your system has internet connectivity and exposes web services, you can immediately offer additional value-added services.

SSL Proxy Service (Upsell Opportunity): Your devices expose local HTTP interfaces for configuration and monitoring. Many customers need secure remote access to these interfaces. Offer SSL proxy service as an additional product.

Service implementation options:

- **Balena integration:** Built-in secure tunneling with device management
- **Custom proxy service:** Deploy your own reverse proxy infrastructure
- **Third-party solutions:** ngrok, localtunnel, or similar services

Business model benefits:

- Monthly recurring revenue from proxy service
- Increased device stickiness through value-added services
- Customer support becomes easier with remote access capability
- Upselling opportunity during initial device configuration

4.8.2 Additional Upsell Services

Remote monitoring and analytics:

- Device health monitoring with alerting
- Usage analytics and reporting dashboards
- Predictive maintenance notifications
- Performance optimization recommendations

Enhanced support services:

- Remote diagnostics and troubleshooting
- Automatic software updates with rollback capability
- 24/7 monitoring with incident response
- Priority technical support queue

These services transform one-time hardware sales into ongoing customer relationships with predictable recurring revenue.

Key differences from POC to production software:

Aspect	POC	Production
Error Handling	Print and exit	Graceful recovery
Logging	Debug to console	Structured, minimal
Configuration	Hardcoded values	External config files
Updates	Manual reinstall	Automated remote updates
Monitoring	Manual observation	Automated health checks
Network	Simple WiFi	Fallback mechanisms
Storage	SQLite files	Redis with persistence

Tabela 4.1: POC vs Production software comparison

Production software requires systematic approach to reliability, maintainability, and supportability. Every component must handle failures gracefully and provide visibility into system health. The investment in robust software architecture pays dividends in reduced support costs and increased customer satisfaction.

5

KEY CHECKLIST FOR PRODUCTION CODE

WRITING CODE FOR PRODUCTION devices is fundamentally different from hobbyist projects or internal tools. When your code ships to customers who expect commercial-grade reliability, every design decision becomes critical. A single oversight can result in thousands of field service calls or, worse, a completely failed product launch.

After shipping over 5,000 devices and dealing with the consequences of poor production code decisions, I've learned these lessons the hard way. This chapter distills the most critical considerations for production-ready code.

5.1 REMOTE UPDATE CAPABILITY

Always implement remote update functionality from day one.

You will need to update your devices. Not might need—will need. Whether it's fixing a critical bug, adding a customer-requested feature, or simply changing the font size in the UI, the ability to update deployed devices remotely is non-negotiable.

Real Crisis: Time Calculation Bug

I discovered a critical bug in my time attendance recorder that incorrectly calculated overtime hours in specific edge cases—when employees clocked in exactly at midnight during daylight saving time transitions. The bug affected payroll calculations for dozens of companies. Without remote update capability, I would have had to physically visit hundreds of deployed devices or face potential lawsuits and complete reputation destruction. The remote update saved my business.

Minor Issues Add Up

Even seemingly trivial updates matter. A client once threatened to cancel a 500-unit order because they couldn't read the status display—the font was too small for their environment. Without remote update capability, I would have faced the choice between losing the client or manually visiting 50+ already-deployed devices to flash new firmware.

Implementation considerations:

- Use cryptographically signed updates to prevent tampering (e.g., using GPG signatures, x.509 certificates. Could be even git pull based)
- Implement rollback mechanisms for failed updates (e.g., using versioned firmware, A/B OTA updates)
- Design your update system before writing application code

- Test the update process extensively—it's harder to fix than the original code
- **Consider Balena Cloud:** Provides enterprise-grade remote update capability out of the box

5.2 SSH Access Strategy

Plan your support access carefully, considering both security and customer constraints.

SSH access for support is essential, but many corporate environments block SSH traffic or restrict open ports. You need a support strategy that works within your customers' security policies.

Options to consider:

1. **Custom SSH port:** Use non-standard ports (e.g., 2222, 8022) to avoid basic port blocking
2. **Customer-triggered access:** Implement a mechanism where customers can temporarily enable SSH when support is needed
3. **Reverse SSH tunnels:** Device initiates connection to your support server
4. **VPN solutions:** Tools like Balena or custom VPN implementations
5. **Balena Cloud SSH:** Provides secure SSH access through their cloud infrastructure, bypassing firewall restrictions

> **Real-World Constraint**
>
> Enterprise customers often have strict firewall policies. Plan your support access strategy during the design phase, not when you're desperately trying to troubleshoot a failing device in production.

5.3 Operating System Selection

Choose your OS foundation carefully—this decision affects everything else.

For Raspberry Pi devices, you have several paths:

5.3.1 Custom Raspbian Build

Build your own minimal OS using pi-gen: `https://github.com/RPi-Distro/pi-gen`

Advantages:

- Complete control over included packages
- Smaller attack surface
- Faster boot times
- Reproducible builds

Disadvantages:

- Significant initial setup time
- You're responsible for security updates
- Limited ecosystem support

5.3.2 Balena OS Alternative

Balena provides a complete IoT device management platform with both paid and open-source options.

Balena Cloud (Paid):

- Out-of-the-box device management
- Automatic updates and monitoring
- Professional support
- Docker-based application deployment
- **Built-in remote update capability:** Push updates to devices worldwide with a single command

OpenBalena (Open Source):

- Self-hosted device management
- No ongoing costs
- Full control over infrastructure

> **Balena Gotchas**
>
> **Certification Issues:** Balena certificates can expire, potentially breaking device connectivity.
> **Always-On VPN:** Even when disabled, the VPN infrastructure remains present, which some security-conscious customers reject.
> **Driver Limitations:** Custom hardware drivers can be challenging to integrate into Balena's Docker ecosystem.
> **Docker Overhead:** Additional resource usage may impact performance on resource-constrained devices.

Despite these limitations, Balena works exceptionally well for most use cases and can significantly reduce development time.

5.4 Multiple Connectivity Options

Always provide at least two ways to connect to your device.

Network connectivity is the most common point of failure in deployed devices. Customers will find themselves in situations where their primary connection method fails.

Proven combinations:

- **Ethernet + WiFi:** Most reliable for stationary installations
- **WiFi + Bluetooth:** Useful for mobile or temporary deployments
- **Ethernet + Bluetooth:** Good for environments with WiFi restrictions

In my time attendance device "Skryba,"I implemented WiFi + Bluetooth networking. When customers had WiFi connectivity issues, they could still configure and operate the device via Bluetooth using a mobile app.

5.5 Zero-Configuration User Experience

Customers are not developers—design for plug-and-play operation.

Your device should work immediately upon power-up, requiring minimal configuration. Implement zero-configuration networking protocols and automatic device discovery.

Key principles:

- Default to automatic IP configuration (DHCP)
- Broadcast device presence (mDNS/Bonjour)

- Provide web-based configuration interface
- Use QR codes for easy mobile device pairing
- Implement status LEDs for non-technical troubleshooting

5.6 Power Supply Considerations

Assume inconsistent power quality and implement atomic operations.

Customer power supplies are often unreliable. I once had a client whose device constantly shut down unexpectedly due to insufficient power supply capacity. Your code must handle sudden power loss gracefully.

Critical practices:

- Use atomic file operations for critical data
- Implement transaction logs for multi-step operations
- Design state machines that can recover from any interruption
- Consider using a supercapacitor for graceful shutdown detection

5.7 Hardware Boundary Enforcement

Explicitly limit supported hardware configurations.

If you support HDMI output, specify exactly which resolutions you support. In my experience, stating ï1920×1080 onlyp̈revents countless support issues with customers using unusual display configurations.

Common boundaries to enforce:

- Display resolutions and refresh rates
- Network interface speeds
- Storage device types and sizes
- USB device classes
- Camera resolutions and frame rates

5.8 Automatic Recovery Mechanisms

Implement comprehensive auto-recovery for all failure modes.

Customers expect devices to handle problems automatically without manual intervention.

Recovery strategies:

- **Application crash:** Automatic restart with exponential backoff
- **Network disconnection:** Automatic reconnection with fallback methods
- **Memory exhaustion:** Automatic reboot when available memory drops below threshold
- **Disk full:** Automatic log rotation and cleanup of temporary files

Watchdog Implementation

```
#!/bin/bash
# Simple application watchdog
while true; do
    if ! pgrep -f "my_application" > /dev/null; then
        echo "Application not running, restarting..."
        /opt/myapp/start_application.sh
        sleep 30
    fi
    sleep 10
done
```

5.9 Credential Security

Never hardcode credentials that could compromise the entire application.

This includes API keys, database passwords, encryption keys, and any authentication tokens. Hardcoded credentials create a single point of failure that affects all deployed devices.

Secure alternatives:

- Device-specific certificates generated during manufacturing
- Runtime credential provisioning through secure channels
- Hardware security modules (HSM) for key storage
- Encrypted credential storage with device-unique keys

5.10 Local Security

Secure all endpoints, even on local networks.

Never expose password-unprotected endpoints, even on supposedly "trusted"local networks. Local networks are often less secure than public internet connections.

Minimum security measures:

- Authentication required for all administrative functions
- HTTPS for all web interfaces, even local ones
- Input validation on all API endpoints
- Rate limiting to prevent brute-force attacks

5.11 The Embedded Golden Rule

Simpler is always better in embedded systems.

Every additional feature, dependency, or complexity point increases the probability of failure. When in doubt, choose the simpler solution.

Complexity indicators to avoid:

- Multiple programming languages in one project
- Complex dependency chains
- Custom protocols when standard ones exist
- "Smart"features that aren't explicitly requested
- Premature optimization

This principle has saved me more time and customer relationships than any other rule. When facing a choice between an elegant complex solution and a simple working solution, always choose simple.

5.12 Backup All Dependencies

Dependencies disappear without warning. Backup everything (detailed in software chapter).

- Full system images of working configurations
- Complete package caches (APT, pip, npm)
- All external repositories and libraries
- Working Docker containers as archived files

Test regularly: Can you rebuild without internet access?

5.13 Two paths

Always have at least 2 paths - development and production. Push into development first.

5.14 Pre-Deployment Checklist

Before shipping any code update, verify on development path:

1. Remote update mechanism tested and working
2. Support access method confirmed with customer IT
3. All hardcoded values removed or configurable
4. Auto-recovery mechanisms tested with actual failures
5. Security endpoints password-protected
6. Zero-configuration setup tested by non-technical users (ask your relative)

7. Power interruption recovery tested
8. Multiple connectivity methods verified

Following these principles won't eliminate all production issues, but it will dramatically reduce the frequency and severity of field problems. More importantly, it will give you the tools to fix issues remotely when they do occur.

Remember: production code isn't just about making features work—it's about making them work reliably in environments you can't control, for users who aren't experts, with hardware that will inevitably fail in unexpected ways.

And believe me. It's a mess.

6

From spider into first 5 PCB

Your spider prototype works and you've validated the core functionality. Now comes the transition from hand-wired chaos to professional PCB assembly. This chapter covers my process for moving from validated concept to manufactured boards.

I'm not covering PCB design itself - that's a specialized skill best left to professionals. Instead, I focus on the manufacturing process that ensures your boards arrive ready to use.

6.1 The Fundamental Rule: No Manual Soldering

Goal: Make the process completely repeatable without your manual intervention.

Every connector, component, and cable should be professionally assembled at the factory. Manual soldering creates bottlenecks, quality variations, and scaling problems. If you're soldering components yourself, you haven't properly industrialized your process.

Remember that every action is repeated x device you plan to manufacture.

Sometimes is OK to soldier something if you have something simple to set up (for example soldiering 8 gold pins straight - easy peasy, even x100).

6.2 JLCPCB Manufacturing Process

I use JLCPCB (https://jlcpcb.com) for both PCB fabrication and assembly. Their integrated process provides:

PCB + Assembly in one location:

- Order PCB fabrication and component assembly together
- Parts sourced and assembled at their facility
- Complete boards delivered in 5 days
- Repeatable process with consistent quality
- Optional firmware flashing service

Process workflow:

1. Upload PCB design files (Gerbers, pick-and-place, BOM)
2. JLCPCB sources components from their inventory
3. PCB fabrication and assembly happen in parallel
4. Quality testing and packaging
5. Boards ship fully assembled and tested

6.3 Cost Considerations

Real JLCPCB cost example (10 boards - 2 designs):

Item	**Cost**
PCB Prototype - Basic (5pcs)	$2.01
Economic PCBA - Basic (5pcs)	$34.58
PCB Prototype - Ethernet (5pcs)	$7.06
Economic PCBA - Ethernet (5pcs)	$47.91
Merchandise Total	$91.56
Shipping Charge	$53.94
Customs duties & taxes	$39.26
Order Total	**$184.76**

Tabela 6.1: Actual JLCPCB order - 2 board variants (10 total boards)

Key observations from real pricing:

- Two board designs: basic version and version with Ethernet connector
- PCB fabrication cost minimal ($9.07 total for both designs)
- Assembly costs vary by complexity: $34.58 vs $47.91 for Ethernet version
- Shipping ($53.94) exceeds merchandise cost - typical for small batches
- Duties and taxes ($39.26) add 43% overhead
- **Average cost per board: $18.48 for 10 boards across 2 designs**

Design complexity impact: The Ethernet version costs 39% more in assembly ($47.91 vs $34.58), demonstrating how additional components directly affect manufacturing cost. Plan component count carefully during design phase.

6.4 Custom Cables Integration

Minimize field assembly by using professional cable assemblies from LCSC Custom Cables (https://www.lcsc.com/customcables).

Cable strategy:

- Design board-to-board connections with standard connectors
- Specify exact cable lengths and connector types
- Include strain relief and proper jacketing
- Order cables with boards for integrated delivery

Result: Final assembly becomes "connect cable A to connector B"rather than wire stripping and soldering.

6.5 Design for Assembly (DFA)

Your PCB design must accommodate automated assembly:

Component placement considerations:

- All SMD components on one side when possible
- Adequate spacing for pick-and-place equipment
- Through-hole components minimized or eliminated
- Test points accessible for automated testing

Connector strategy:

- Use JLCPCB's component library when possible
- Standard connector families (JST, Molex, TE)
- Avoid custom or hard-to-source connectors
- Include mounting hardware in assembly

6.6 Version Control and Documentation

Version every PCB iteration systematically:

PCB Version Control Example

Project naming convention:

- TimeAttendance_v1.0 - Initial prototype
- TimeAttendance_v1.1 - Component value fixes
- TimeAttendance_v2.0 - Layout changes
- TimeAttendance_v2.1 - Manufacturing optimization

Cloud storage structure:

```
/TimeAttendance_PCB/
  /v1.0/
    /design_files/
    /assembly_docs/
    /test_results/
  /v1.1/
    /design_files/
    /assembly_docs/
    /test_results/
```

Documentation requirements for each version:

- Complete design files (schematic, layout, Gerbers)
- Bill of Materials with part numbers
- Assembly drawings and instructions
- Test procedures and acceptance criteria
- Change log from previous version

6.7 First 5 PCB Strategy

Order exactly 5 boards for your first iteration:

Board allocation:

- **Board 1:** Immediate functional testing
- **Board 2:** Software development platform
- **Board 3:** Environmental stress testing
- **Board 4:** Customer demonstration unit
- **Board 5:** Archive/backup for troubleshooting

This quantity provides adequate testing capability without excessive cost for changes that will inevitably be needed.

6.8 Quality Validation Process

Upon receiving boards, systematic testing:

1. **Visual inspection:** Component placement, solder quality, damage
2. **Power-on test:** Verify power rails and basic functionality
3. **Interface testing:** All connectors and communication buses
4. **Software deployment:** Load and test application software
5. **Performance validation:** Compare to spider prototype benchmarks

Pass criteria: At least 4 of 5 boards must pass all tests. If fewer pass, investigate root cause before ordering next iteration.

6.9 Common First PCB Issues

Expect these problems on first iteration:

- Component footprint mismatches
- Pin assignment errors
- Inadequate power supply decoupling
- Missing pull-up/pull-down resistors
- Connector pinout mistakes

Design for debugging:

- Include test points for all power rails
- Add LED indicators for major functions
- Provide jumpers for configuration changes
- Include serial debug connector

6.10 Preparing for Next Iteration

Document everything learned from first PCB batch:

Technical changes needed:

- Component value adjustments
- Layout improvements
- Additional features required
- Manufacturing feedback incorporation

Process improvements:

- Assembly time reduction opportunities
- Test procedure refinements
- Documentation clarity issues
- Cost optimization possibilities

The first PCB iteration validates electrical design and manufacturing processes. Expect significant changes before the second iteration, which will focus on mechanical integration and production optimization.

6.11 Success Metrics

First PCB iteration is successful if:

- Basic functionality matches spider prototype performance
- Manufacturing process is repeatable and documented
- Assembly time is predictable and reasonable
- Cost projections align with business model
- Quality issues are identifiable and correctable

The goal isn't perfection - it's systematic validation of your transition from prototype to manufactured product. Each iteration should solve specific, documented problems while maintaining overall functionality.

7
Key checklist for production hardware

Your PCB arrived from manufacturing and basic functionality works. But working once in ideal conditions doesn't mean production-ready. This chapter provides systematic validation criteria to determine if your hardware is ready for real-world deployment.

Production hardware must survive conditions you never considered during development. Customer environments are harsh, unpredictable, and unforgiving. Every weakness will be discovered and exploited by normal usage.

7.1 Stability and Reliability Testing

7.1.1 Continuous Operation Test

Requirement: Run for at least 5 days without interruption.

Set up your board to run your complete application continuously for 120 hours minimum. Monitor for:

- System crashes or reboots
- Memory leaks causing degraded performance
- Temperature-induced failures
- Network connectivity issues
- Storage corruption or filesystem errors

Pass criteria: Zero unplanned restarts, stable performance metrics throughout test period.

> **Real-World Example**
>
> Our time attendance system would mysteriously fail after 72 hours of continuous operation. The issue turned out to be a memory leak in the RFID polling loop - a bug that only manifested under sustained operation. Lab testing caught this before customer deployment.

7.2 Connector and Serviceability Validation

7.2.1 Connector Replaceability

Requirement: Connectors must be serviceable and replaceable.

Test every external connector:

- Disconnect and reconnect each connector 50 times minimum
- Verify positive retention and proper seating
- Confirm connectors can be replaced without specialized tools

- Test with slight misalignment - connectors should guide properly

7.2.2 Supply Chain Backup Plan

Requirement: Clear replacement path for every component.
Document for each critical component:

- Primary supplier part number
- At least two alternative suppliers
- Compatible substitute part numbers
- Lead time expectations for each option
- Pricing differences between alternatives

This documentation becomes critical when your primary supplier discontinues parts or experiences supply disruptions.

7.3 Mechanical Integration

7.3.1 Enclosure Fit Verification

Requirement: Board must fit properly in intended enclosure.
Physical validation checklist:

- PCB mounting holes align with enclosure posts
- Adequate clearance around all components
- Connector access through enclosure openings
- No interference between PCB and enclosure features
- Proper strain relief for external cables

Tolerance consideration: Account for manufacturing variations in both PCB and enclosure dimensions.

7.4 Comprehensive Interface Testing

7.4.1 Assume Nothing Works

Requirement: Test every peripheral and interface explicitly.

Do not assume USB ports work because the schematic looks correct. Test systematically:

USB Interface Testing:

- Test with different USB device classes (storage, HID, CDC)
- Verify power delivery meets USB specifications
- Test hot-plug insertion and removal
- Confirm data transfer rates meet expectations

Network Interface Testing:

- Ethernet link negotiation at different speeds
- WiFi connection to various router types
- Network reconnection after cable disconnect
- Performance under network congestion

GPIO and Serial Interfaces:

- Voltage level verification with oscilloscope
- Signal timing and setup/hold requirements
- Electrical loading effects with connected peripherals
- EMI susceptibility with nearby switching circuits

7.5 Power Supply Stress Testing

7.5.1 Multi-Vendor Power Supply Validation

Requirement: Test with at least 3 different power supplies.

Power supply variations can reveal marginal designs:

Test Configuration 1: 3A Supply

- Verify adequate current capacity under peak load
- Monitor voltage regulation during load transients
- Test power-on sequencing and brown-out behavior

Test Configuration 2: 2.5A Supply

- Validate operation at minimum recommended current
- Confirm no false triggering of protection circuits
- Test behavior when approaching current limit

Test Configuration 3: Different Vendor

- Verify compatibility with alternative supply architecture
- Test with different connector types if applicable
- Validate any proprietary communication protocols

Power Supply Reality Check

Customer power supplies are often inadequate or degraded. Design for 20% margin above calculated requirements. I've seen "5V 2A"adapters that barely delivered 1.5A under load, causing mysterious system instabilities.

7.6 Display and Video Output Testing

7.6.1 Monitor Compatibility Validation

Requirement: Test HDMI output with multiple monitor types.
If your system includes video output, test with diverse displays:
Monitor Type Variations:

- Different screen resolutions (1080p, 4K, older formats)
- Various manufacturers (Dell, Samsung, LG, generic)
- Different HDMI cable lengths (1m, 3m, 5m)
- Monitors with different EDID implementations

Validation criteria:

- Automatic resolution detection works reliably
- Display initializes within 10 seconds of power-on
- No visual artifacts or timing issues
- Hot-plug detection functions correctly

7.7 Thermal Management Validation

7.7.1 Enclosed Operation Testing

Requirement: Test thermal performance in realistic enclosure.
Create a test enclosure that simulates final product conditions:
Thermal stress test procedure:

1. Enclose board in representative housing

2. Run CPU-intensive application for sustained period
3. Monitor component temperatures with thermal camera
4. Verify no thermal throttling occurs during normal operation
5. Test in ambient temperatures expected in deployment

Temperature monitoring points:

- CPU/SoC surface temperature
- Power supply regulator temperatures
- Connector junction temperatures
- Ambient air temperature inside enclosure

Pass criteria: All components remain within manufacturer specifications during continuous operation.

7.8 Data Integrity and Documentation

7.8.1 File Management Requirements

Requirement: Complete backup of production files. Maintain version-controlled archive including:

- PCB design files (native format and Gerbers)
- Bill of materials with exact part numbers
- Assembly drawings and procedures
- Test specifications and acceptance criteria

- Software versions deployed to boards

Backup verification: Periodically verify that archived files can recreate identical boards.

7.8.2 Assembly Minimization

Requirement: Minimize field soldering to absolute minimum.

Production-ready hardware should require minimal manual assembly:

Acceptable manual operations:

- Connecting pre-manufactured cable assemblies
- Installing into enclosure with screws
- Applying labels or protective films

Unacceptable manual operations:

- Soldering wires to PCB in field
- Modifying components during assembly
- Hand-tuning or calibration procedures
- Complex cable routing or strain relief creation

7.9 Production Readiness Checklist

Before declaring hardware production-ready, verify every item:

1. ✓5-day continuous operation test passed
2. ✓All connectors tested for replaceability
3. ✓Component substitution plan documented

4. ✓Enclosure fit confirmed with tolerances
5. ✓Every interface tested with real peripherals
6. ✓Multiple power supply configurations validated
7. ✓HDMI/display compatibility verified with diverse monitors
8. ✓Thermal performance validated in enclosed configuration
9. ✓Complete file backup and version control implemented
10. ✓Manual assembly minimized to acceptable operations

7.10 Failure Mode Analysis

Document how the system behaves when things go wrong:

Power failure scenarios:

- Sudden power loss during operation
- Undervoltage conditions
- Power supply overcurrent protection activation

Communication failure scenarios:

- Network cable disconnection
- WiFi signal loss
- USB device hot removal

Environmental stress scenarios:

- Operation at temperature extremes

- High humidity conditions
- Mechanical vibration or shock

Understanding failure modes allows you to design appropriate recovery mechanisms and set realistic customer expectations.

Production hardware isn't just hardware that works - it's hardware that works reliably in conditions you didn't anticipate, with components you can actually source, assembled by processes you can scale, and documented well enough that someone else can manufacture it identically.

8
Select case

Your PCB is validated and software development is underway. Now comes a critical decision that affects manufacturing cost, assembly complexity, and market perception: selecting or designing the enclosure.

The case decision impacts every aspect of production - from assembly time to shipping costs to customer perception of quality. Choose wrong and you'll face expensive redesigns or manufacturing complications.

8.1 Standard vs. Custom Enclosure Decision

8.1.1 Existing Standard Cases

Kradex and established manufacturers offer proven solutions:

- Immediate availability with known dimensions
- Lower upfront cost - no tooling investment

- Proven durability and regulatory compliance
- Multiple mounting options typically available
- Standardized assembly processes

When to choose standard cases:

- Production volume under 500 units
- PCB can be designed to fit standard dimensions
- No unusual interface or mounting requirements
- Fast time-to-market priority
- Limited development budget

8.1.2 Custom Case Development

Design your own enclosure when:

- Unique form factor provides competitive advantage
- Standard cases don't accommodate your interfaces
- Production volume justifies tooling investment
- Brand differentiation requires custom appearance

8.2 3D Printing Technology Selection

8.2.1 The Professional Standard: MJF

Multi Jet Fusion (MJF) is the only professional 3D printing option.

Avoid these inferior technologies:

- **FDM/FFF:** Layer lines visible, poor surface finish, mechanical weakness
- **Resin printing:** Toxic materials, poor durability, surface quality issues
- **SLA:** Expensive, limited materials, post-processing complexity

MJF advantages for production prototypes:

- Professional surface finish straight from printer
- Excellent dimensional accuracy and repeatability
- Strong, functional parts suitable for real-world testing
- No visible layer lines or support marks
- Cost-effective for complex geometries

Real MJF prototype costs (Cubic Inch):

Part	Quantity	Cost (EUR)
Bottom enclosure	2 units	€38
Top cover	2 units	€9
Shipping	-	€11
VAT	-	€10
Total order	**4 parts**	**€100**

Tabela 8.1: MJF prototype costs - approximately €50 per complete enclosure including delivery

Material: HP 3D High Reusability PA 12 (Nylon) Tolerance: ±0.3mm Delivery: 6 working days Finish: Dye Black

8.3 Manufacturing Progression Strategy

8.3.1 Three-Stage Development Path

Stage 1: Initial Prototyping (1-5 units) Use any available 3D printing technology for basic fit testing and PCB mounting validation. Quality is secondary to speed and cost at this stage.

Stage 2: Functional Prototypes (5-50 units) Switch to MJF printing for professional appearance and mechanical properties. Use these units for customer demonstrations and extended testing.

Stage 3: Production Decision Point (50+ units) At 50 units sold, evaluate injection molding. The break-even point varies by complexity, but tooling costs typically amortize around 100-500 units.

8.4 Mounting Strategy

8.4.1 Installation Method Planning

Wall mounting considerations:

- Standard wall anchor compatibility
- Cable management and strain relief
- Access to status indicators and interfaces
- Theft resistance and tamper detection
- Level mounting with adjustment capability

Desktop device requirements:

- Stable base preventing tip-over
- Non-slip feet or weighted base
- Cable routing that doesn't interfere with stability
- User interface accessibility and viewing angles

8.4.2 PCB Mounting Methodology

Professional PCB mounting requires precise measurements:

- Use calipers to measure exact PCB dimensions
- Account for component clearance above PCB surface
- Include tolerance for manufacturing variations (±0.2mm typical)
- Verify mounting hole positions with multiple PCB samples
- Design for thermal expansion if operating temperatures vary

Alternative: Hot Glue Mounting

For non-heating devices and low-volume production, hot glue provides acceptable PCB mounting. This eliminates precision machining requirements and accommodates PCB variations. Only suitable when device temperature remains below 60°C.

8.5 Injection Molding Considerations

8.5.1 Always Design with Injection Molding in Mind

Even if starting with 3D printing, design case geometry compatible with injection molding from the beginning. Redesigning for injection molding later is expensive and time-consuming.

Injection mold-friendly design principles:

- **Keep it simple:** Minimize complex geometries and undercuts
- **Uniform wall thickness:** Typically 1.5-3mm for electronics enclosures
- **Draft angles:** 1-2 degrees minimum on all vertical surfaces
- **Avoid thin features:** Minimum feature size depends on material choice
- **Split line planning:** Consider where mold halves separate

8.5.2 Injection Molding Timeline

Recommended progression:

1. **1-5 units:** Any 3D printing for basic validation
2. **5-50 units:** MJF printing for professional appearance
3. **50+ units sold:** Evaluate injection molding economics
4. **1000+ units planned:** Injection molding becomes cost-effective

Fullbax Formy partnership provides established China manufacturing relationships, reducing risk and complexity for European companies entering injection molding.

8.6 Design Simplicity Imperative

8.6.1 Complexity Kills Profitability

Every additional feature, curve, or detail increases manufacturing cost and complexity. Optimize for manufacturability, not aesthetic sophistication.

Cost-driving complexity factors:

- Multiple split lines requiring precision alignment
- Threaded inserts or complex mechanical features
- Multiple materials or overmolding requirements
- Tight tolerances beyond standard manufacturing capability
- Surface textures or decorative elements

Simplicity benefits:

- Lower tooling costs and faster delivery
- Reduced assembly time and labor costs
- Fewer quality control points and failure modes
- Easier inventory management and logistics
- Simplified service and repair procedures

8.7 Case Selection Workflow

8.7.1 Systematic Decision Process

1. **Define requirements:** Interface access, mounting method, environmental conditions
2. **Survey standard options:** Evaluate Kradex and similar catalogs
3. **PCB fit analysis:** Can board be designed to fit standard enclosure?
4. **Cost comparison:** Standard case + PCB redesign vs. custom tooling
5. **Volume projection:** Realistic sales forecast over 2-year period
6. **Prototype with cheapest option:** Validate assumptions before committing
7. **Scale manufacturing method:** Progress through 3D printing to injection molding

8.8 Quality and Durability Testing

8.8.1 Enclosure Validation Requirements

Mechanical testing:

- Drop testing from 1-meter height (simulate installation accidents)
- Connector insertion/removal cycling (500+ cycles minimum)

- Environmental stress testing (temperature, humidity cycling)
- UV exposure testing for outdoor or window-mounted devices

Thermal performance:

- Internal temperature monitoring during extended operation
- Hot spot identification using thermal imaging
- Ventilation effectiveness measurement
- Component derating analysis based on actual temperatures

8.9 Common Case Selection Mistakes

Overengineering aesthetic appeal: Complex curves and features dramatically increase cost without improving functionality.

Ignoring assembly labor: Cases requiring extensive manual assembly increase per-unit cost and quality variation.

Premature injection molding: Committing to tooling before validating market demand and design stability.

Inadequate thermal planning: Failing to account for heat generation in enclosed operation.

Poor cable management: Not planning strain relief and connector access during case design.

Remember: the best case is the simplest one that meets functional requirements and scales cost-effectively with production volume. Aesthetic sophistication should never compromise manufacturability or profitability.

9
Certification

Certification requirements can make or break your product launch timeline and budget. This chapter covers the essential certifications needed to legally sell electronic devices, based on practical experience navigating regulatory requirements.

Different products require vastly different certification approaches. I always outsource certification to professionals because the requirements vary dramatically by application. Time attendance devices need LVD, CE, and radio certifications. Cybertap requires food safety compliance since it touches beverages. Smart helmets involve fire safety, battery regulations, and explosion-proof requirements. Each application domain brings unique regulatory challenges that require specialized expertise.

9.1 Understanding CE Marking Self-Declaration

> **CE Marking Reality**
>
> The CE marking is applied by the manufacturer - that's you. By affixing the CE mark, you declare that according to your knowledge, the product meets the conditions for CE marking. You determine the scope and type of appropriate testing required. However, you bear full responsibility for the product - if someone later proves that you marked the product incorrectly, you will face serious legal and financial consequences.

Self-declaration vs. professional testing: While you can technically self-declare CE compliance, this creates enormous liability exposure. Professional testing provides:

- Documented evidence of compliance
- Legal protection through accredited test reports
- Technical expertise in identifying potential issues
- Insurance coverage for certification errors

The practical reality: You can affix CE marking yourself, but you really should conduct proper testing through accredited laboratories. The cost of testing is minimal compared to the potential liability of incorrect self-declaration.

9.2 Why Certification Matters

Legal requirements for market access:

- Cannot legally sell electronic devices without proper certification
- Customs authorities can seize non-certified products
- Liability exposure increases dramatically without compliance
- Major distributors and retailers require certification documentation
- Insurance claims may be denied for non-certified products

Timeline impact: Certification processes can add 3-6 months to your product launch timeline. Plan certification activities in parallel with final product development, not as an afterthought.

9.3 Common Certification Requirements

9.3.1 European Union - CE Marking

Required for all electronic devices sold in EU:

- EMC Directive (electromagnetic compatibility)
- Low Voltage Directive (electrical safety)
- RED Directive (radio equipment) - if device has wireless capabilities
- RoHS Directive (restriction of hazardous substances)

Cost estimates: €5,000 - €15,000 for basic electronic devices
Timeline: 4-8 weeks for testing, additional time for documentation

9.3.2 United States - FCC Certification

FCC requirements vary by device type:

- Class B digital devices (most consumer electronics)
- Intentional radiators (WiFi, Bluetooth devices)
- Unintentional radiators (devices with digital circuits)

Cost estimates: $3,000 - $12,000 depending on complexity **Timeline:** 3-6 weeks for testing

9.3.3 Safety Certifications

UL/ETL certification for US market: Required for devices with AC power connections or specific safety-critical applications.

IEC standards compliance: International safety standards that form basis for many national requirements.

9.4 When to Start Certification Process

Certification timeline integration:

Development Stage	Certification Action
Spider prototype	Research applicable standards
First PCB iteration	Consult with certification lab
Second PCB iteration	Pre-compliance testing
Production-ready hardware	Full certification testing

Tabela 9.1: Certification timeline integration

Pre-compliance testing value: Conduct informal testing with certification lab before final certification. This identifies issues early when fixes are still economical.

9.5 Certification Strategy

9.5.1 Professional Guidance Required

Engage certification specialists early:

- Certification labs provide consulting on applicable standards
- Product design decisions affect certification complexity and cost
- Some design choices can make certification impossible or prohibitively expensive
- Professional guidance prevents costly redesigns

Don't attempt DIY certification: The regulatory landscape is complex and constantly evolving. Professional certification services are essential for commercial products.

9.5.2 Common Certification Challenges

EMC (Electromagnetic Compatibility) issues:

- Poor PCB layout causing radiation emissions
- Inadequate filtering on power and signal lines
- Cable routing and shielding problems
- Enclosure design affecting electromagnetic performance

Safety standard compliance:

- Improper spacing between high and low voltage circuits
- Inadequate protection against electric shock

- Component ratings insufficient for application
- Missing safety markings and documentation

9.6 Design for Certification

9.6.1 Certification-Friendly Design Practices

PCB design considerations:

- Proper ground plane design
- Adequate filtering on all power inputs
- Appropriate trace routing and spacing
- Component selection for EMC performance

Enclosure design impact:

- Conductive enclosures may help with EMC
- Cable entry points affect shielding effectiveness
- Ventilation requirements vs. electromagnetic containment
- Access requirements for testing and inspection

9.7 Cost Planning

Certification budget planning:
Additional costs to consider:

- Travel expenses for testing at certification labs
- Potential redesign costs if initial testing fails

Certification Type	**EU (EUR)**	**US (USD)**
Basic EMC testing	3,000 - 7,000	2,000 - 5,000
Safety certification	5,000 - 10,000	3,000 - 8,000
Wireless certification	8,000 - 15,000	5,000 - 12,000
Total estimate	**16,000 - 32,000**	**10,000 - 25,000**

Tabela 9.2: Certification cost estimates for typical IoT device

- Documentation preparation and technical file creation
- Annual surveillance costs for some certifications

9.8 Component Certification vs. Product Certification

Critical Misconception: Component CE !

Having CE-marked components does not automatically grant CE marking to your assembled product. Each component's individual compliance contributes to overall product compliance, but the final system must be tested and certified as a complete unit. You cannot simply combine CE-marked parts and declare the product CE compliant.

Why component certification isn't enough:

- Component interactions can create new EMC issues
- System-level safety requirements differ from component-level
- Enclosure and assembly affect electromagnetic performance

- Cable routing and grounding change electrical characteristics
- Combined power consumption may exceed individual component ratings

Declaration of Conformity documents help significantly: Components like Raspberry Pi Compute Module 4 provide Declaration of Conformity documents that detail their individual compliance status. These documents:

- Specify which standards the component meets
- Define operating conditions and limitations
- Provide technical parameters useful for system-level certification
- Can reduce some testing requirements for the complete product
- Serve as supporting documentation during certification process

Practical approach: Collect Declaration of Conformity documents from all major components (CM4, power supplies, wireless modules). These reduce certification complexity but don't eliminate the need for system-level testing and certification of your complete product.

Critical Change: EPR Registration Required from August 18 2025

Starting August 18, 2025, all manufacturers placing battery-powered devices on the EU market must register for Extended Producer Responsibility (EPR) numbers under EU Regulation 2023/1542. This applies to ANY device containing a battery, including IoT devices, tablets, and portable electronics.

New EPR requirements for battery-containing devices:

- Registration in national producer registers
- EPR number must appear on sales documents, invoices, and online platforms
- Applies to all EU countries - each requires separate registration
- Compliance required even for devices exported from EU to other countries
- Covers entire battery lifecycle including sales and disposal

Impact on hardware businesses: This regulation affects virtually all IoT and portable electronic devices. Factor EPR registration costs and administrative overhead into market entry planning for each EU country. The regulation aims to reduce environmental impact throughout battery lifecycle, creating new compliance obligations for hardware manufacturers.

Multi-country compliance: Each EU country maintains separate EPR registration systems. Selling across multiple EU markets requires registration in each target country, significantly increasing administrative complexity for hardware startups.

9.8.1 Market-Specific Requirements

Additional certifications by region:

- **Canada:** ISED certification (similar to FCC)
- **Australia:** ACMA compliance
- **Japan:** TELEC certification for wireless devices
- **China:** CCC certification for many product categories

Market prioritization strategy: Start with primary target markets and expand certification coverage as sales grow. Attempting global certification initially is expensive and often unnecessary.

9.9 Documentation Requirements

9.9.1 Technical File Preparation

Required documentation typically includes:

- Product description and intended use
- Design and manufacturing drawings
- Component specifications and certifications
- Test reports from accredited laboratories
- Risk assessment and safety analysis
- User manual and installation instructions

Documentation maintenance: Certification documentation must be maintained and updated throughout product lifecycle. Changes to design, components, or manufacturing may require re-certification.

9.10 Practical Recommendations

9.10.1 Certification Lab Selection

Choose certification labs based on:

- Accreditation for required standards
- Experience with similar products
- Geographic convenience for testing
- Cost and timeline competitiveness
- Quality of consulting and support services

9.10.2 Timeline and Project Management

Critical path considerations:

- Certification often becomes critical path for product launch
- Plan for potential re-testing if initial attempts fail
- Consider seasonal laboratory capacity (busy periods)
- Maintain buffer time in launch schedule for certification delays

9.11 When Things Go Wrong

Common failure scenarios:

- EMC emissions exceed limits - requires PCB or enclosure redesign
- Safety spacing violations - may require component relocation

- Documentation inadequacies - delays while correcting technical files
- Component non-compliance - sourcing certified replacement parts

Mitigation strategies:

- Build certification risk into project timeline and budget
- Establish relationships with certification labs early
- Consider certification requirements during design phase
- Maintain detailed documentation throughout development

9.12 Key Takeaways

Certification is a necessary but complex aspect of hardware product development. The regulatory landscape requires professional expertise to navigate successfully. Budget adequate time and money for certification, and engage with certification specialists early in your development process.

Most importantly: don't let certification be an afterthought. Design decisions made early in development significantly impact certification cost, timeline, and success probability. Professional guidance during design phase is far more cost-effective than redesigning for certification compliance later.

10

FIRST 100 BOARDS

THIS IS THE MOMENT that transforms your project from an engineering exercise into a real business. You've validated your design with 5 boards, refined the software, confirmed the enclosure fit, and now you're ready to scale to 100 units. This is my favorite phase in the entire device development process—when proper preparation meets systematic execution.

If you've followed the systematic approach from previous chapters, this phase should feel almost anticlimactic. That's exactly what you want—manufacturing should be boring, predictable, and repeatable.

10.1 THE BEAUTIFUL SIMPLICITY OF REPLICATION

When everything is properly prepared, scaling to 100 units becomes a series of simple clicks:

Step 1: JLCPCB Reorder Log into your JLCPCB account and find your validated PCB order. Click "Reorder"and change quantity from 5 to 100 pieces. The beauty of this moment is that everything else remains identical—same Gerber files, same components, same assembly process.

> **Component Availability Check**
>
> Before clicking "Place Order," verify component availability. JLCPCB will flag any out-of-stock components. If substitutions are needed, this is your last chance to validate them against your tested design.

Step 2: Case Manufacturing Contact your enclosure partner (Cubic Inch for 3D printing or your injection molding supplier) and request 100 cases. If you've been using MJF printing, this order will likely require 2-3 weeks lead time.

Step 3: Raspberry Pi Procurement Order 100 Compute Module 4 units from Farnell or your established distributor. CM4 availability can be sporadic, so order these immediately after confirming your PCB order.

Step 4: Cable Assembly If using custom cables from LCSC, order 100 sets. Standard cables can be ordered from your regular suppliers.

10.2 Production Organization

Transform your workspace into a mini production line:

10.2.1 Inventory Management

Shelf Organization Strategy:

- **Shelf 1:** Incoming PCBs (sorted by batch and test status)
- **Shelf 2:** Enclosures and mechanical components
- **Shelf 3:** Raspberry Pi modules and accessories

- **Shelf 4:** Cable assemblies and consumables
- **Shelf 5:** Completed devices ready for testing
- **Shelf 6:** Tested and packaged units ready for shipping

Component tracking: Use simple spreadsheet or paper checklist to track inventory consumption and identify shortages before they halt production.

10.2.2 First 10 Devices Test Run

Before committing to full production, build 10 complete devices using your production process:

Assembly validation checklist:

1. PCB-to-case fit verification (all 10 boards)
2. Connector accessibility and cable routing
3. Assembly time measurement per unit
4. Quality consistency across the batch
5. Functional testing of complete assemblies

Time measurement importance: Document assembly time for these 10 units. This data determines your production capacity and labor costs for future orders.

10.3 Quality Assurance at Scale

10.3.1 Testing Protocol for 100 Units

You cannot functionally test every unit like you did with 5 prototypes. Implement statistical sampling:

Testing strategy:

- **Visual inspection:** 100% of units (quick PCB assembly check)
- **Power-on test:** 100% of units (basic functionality verification)
- **Full functional test:** 20% of units (detailed feature validation)
- **Burn-in testing:** 10% of units (24-hour continuous operation)

10.3.2 Defect Management

Plan for 2-5% defect rate even with proven components:

Common issues at 100-unit scale:

- Component placement variations
- Solder joint quality inconsistencies
- Case manufacturing tolerances
- CM4 module failures (rare but possible)

Defect resolution process:

1. Document all failures with photos and symptoms
2. Categorize issues (PCB assembly vs. component vs. software)
3. Repair what's economical, scrap what's not
4. Update assembly procedures based on failure patterns

10.4 Production Metrics and Learning

10.4.1 Key Performance Indicators

Track these metrics for your 100-unit run:

Metric	Target
Assembly time per unit	15-30 minutes
First-pass yield rate	>95%
Rework rate	<5%
Scrap rate	<2%
Software flash success	100%

Tabela 10.1: Production targets for 100-unit run

Assembly time breakdown example:

- CM4 installation: 2 minutes
- Cable connections: 3 minutes
- Enclosure assembly: 5 minutes
- Software installation: 8 minutes
- Quality verification: 7 minutes
- **Total: 25 minutes per unit**

10.4.2 Cost Analysis Reality Check

Document actual costs vs. projections:

Real cost breakdown (example):

- PCB + assembly: €18.50 per unit

- Enclosure: €12.00 per unit
- CM4 module: €35.00 per unit
- Cables and accessories: €8.00 per unit
- Labor (25 min @ €20/hour): €8.33 per unit
- **Total manufacturing cost: €81.83 per unit**

10.5 Software Deployment at Scale

10.5.1 CM4 Programming Infrastructure

Manual software installation doesn't scale to 100 units. For Compute Module 4 devices, you need reliable eMMC programming capability.

CM4/CM5 Programmer Essential Tool: The CM4/CM5 Programmer (https://shop.razniewski.eu/p/cm4prog) becomes critical at this scale. This compact programmer provides professional-grade functionality for batch operations:

- Support for both CM4 and CM5 modules
- Automatic eMMC boot mode switching (no manual jumpers)
- Single USB connection for power and data
- Convenient cutout for easy module insertion/removal
- Designed specifically for mass production workflows

Production programming workflow:

1. Insert CM4 module into programmer

2. Switch programmer to "BOOT"mode (ON position)
3. Connect USB cable to computer
4. Run `usbboot` to detect eMMC as USB drive
5. Flash production image using standard disk imaging tools
6. Switch programmer to "RUN"mode (1 position)
7. Power cycle - module boots from flashed eMMC
8. Remove programmed module and install in carrier board

Automated provisioning strategy: Configure your production image for automatic internet registration:

- Include unique device identifier generation script
- Implement first-boot internet connectivity check
- Design automatic software download and configuration
- Include fallback mechanism for offline scenarios

> **Programming Efficiency**
>
> With the CM4/CM5 Programmer, you can process 10-15 modules per hour including image flashing and verification. The automatic boot mode switching eliminates manual jumper manipulation, reducing errors and speeding production. For 100 units, plan 6-8 hours of dedicated programming work.

Production image design: Create a base image that handles device-specific configuration automatically:

- Generate unique device serial numbers on first boot
- Connect to internet and register device identity

- Download customer-specific configuration and software updates
- Create local backup of configuration for offline operation
- Enable remote update capability for future maintenance

10.5.2 Automated Installation Process

Image preparation strategy:

- Create master image with all software pre-installed
- Include device-specific configuration scripts
- Implement first-boot configuration automation
- Test image thoroughly on multiple modules before batch programming

> **Programming Efficiency**
>
> With proper setup, the CM4 Programmer enables programming 10-15 modules per hour. For 100 units, plan a full day of dedicated programming work. Having a second programmer allows parallel operations and backup capability.

10.6 Common 100-Unit Production Challenges

10.6.1 Supply Chain Hiccups

Component shortage scenarios:

- CM4 modules backordered (plan 4-6 week buffer stock)

- JLCPCB component substitutions (validate electrical compatibility)
- Case manufacturing delays (order cases first, longest lead time)
- Custom cable delivery issues (maintain backup standard cable option)

10.6.2 Quality Issues

Batch-related problems:

- PCB assembly quality variation between production runs
- Case dimensional tolerance stack-up issues
- Component lot-to-lot performance variations
- Software compatibility issues with newer OS versions

> **Critical Success Factor**
>
> The key to successful 100-unit production is having solved all fundamental problems during the 5-unit phase. Production scaling amplifies both successes and failures. Any issue that occurs 1-in-5 during prototyping will occur 20 times in your 100-unit run.

10.7 Preparing for the Next Scale

10.7.1 Lessons Learned Documentation

Document everything learned during 100-unit production:

Process improvements identified:

- Assembly sequence optimizations
- Quality check procedure refinements
- Supplier performance evaluations
- Cost reduction opportunities

Design improvements for next revision:

- Component placement optimizations
- Connector accessibility improvements
- Test point additions for production testing
- Assembly-friendly design modifications

10.7.2 Scaling Decision Point

After successfully producing 100 units, evaluate scaling options:
Next production volume decisions:

- **200-500 units:** Refine current process, minimal tooling changes
- **500-1000 units:** Consider injection molding for enclosures
- **1000+ units:** Evaluate contract manufacturing partnerships

10.8 The Satisfaction of Systematic Success

The 100-unit milestone represents validation of your entire development process. When you can click "Reorder"on JLCPCB and confidently scale production 20x, you've achieved something significant.

This phase proves that hardware entrepreneurship isn't about heroic engineering efforts—it's about systematic problem-solving, careful validation, and methodical scaling. The excitement comes not from technical complexity, but from the elegant simplicity of replication.

You've transformed an idea into a repeatable manufacturing process. That's the foundation of every successful hardware business.

Success indicators for 100-unit production:

- Assembly time consistent across all units
- Quality issues resolved through process improvements, not heroic debugging
- Customer orders fulfilled on predictable timelines
- Inventory management under control
- Profit margins align with business model projections

The next chapter covers the systematic documentation of this production process, ensuring that success can be repeated and scaled further.

11
Document process

Documentation is not bureaucracy — it's the difference between a repeatable business and an exhausting personal dependency. After successfully producing your first 100 boards, you have valuable knowledge that must be captured systematically. This chapter covers the two critical purposes of production documentation and how to implement both effectively.

11.1 The Two Pillars of Production Documentation

11.1.1 Purpose 1: Standard Operating Procedures (SOPs)

Goal: Enable anyone to replicate your production process

The test of a proper SOP is simple: can someone with basic technical skills follow your instructions and produce identical results? If your process requires your personal intervention, troubleshooting, or "feel"for the work, you haven't documented it properly.

The monkey test principle: Write procedures detailed enough that someone with minimal experience can execute them successfully. This isn't condescending—it's systematic risk reduction.

11.1.2 Purpose 2: Mistake Analysis and Prevention

Goal: Ensure mistakes happen at most twice

Mistakes are normal and expected. What's unacceptable is repeating the same mistake multiple times. Every error represents a learning opportunity and a process improvement requirement.

The two-strike rule: First occurrence is a mistake. Second occurrence is a learning opportunity. Third occurrence is a process failure.

11.2 Creating Effective SOPs

11.2.1 Organization Prerequisites

Proper SOPs require proper workspace organization. If you've followed the shelf organization strategy from the previous chapter, SOP creation becomes straightforward:

Shelf-based SOPs work because:

- Components have defined locations
- Inventory tracking is visual and immediate
- Assembly sequence follows logical spatial flow
- Quality checkpoints align with physical workflow

11.2.2 Parallelization Strategy

Design SOPs that enable parallel work streams:

SOP 1: Software Preparation

1. CM4 modules from Shelf 3
2. Connect to CM4/CM5 Programmer
3. Switch to BOOT mode, connect USB
4. Flash production image using documented procedure
5. Switch to RUN mode, verify boot
6. Label programmed modules, return to designated Shelf 3 area

SOP 2: Hardware Assembly

1. PCB from Shelf 1 (verified and tested batch)
2. Programmed CM4 from Shelf 3 designated area
3. Install CM4 into PCB following orientation guide
4. Cable assemblies from Shelf 4
5. Connect cables per wiring diagram
6. Enclosure from Shelf 2
7. Assembly into case following mechanical procedure

Result: Two people can work simultaneously, doubling production throughput

11.2.3 SOP Documentation Requirements

Visual documentation hierarchy:

- **Images:** Immediately visible reference for each step
- **Videos:** Detailed guidance when written instructions are insufficient
- **Written procedures:** Step-by-step text instructions with decision points

Image requirements:

- Show correct component orientation
- Highlight connector insertion direction
- Indicate proper cable routing
- Display expected status indicators (LEDs, displays)

Video requirements:

- Demonstrate complex assembly sequences
- Show proper handling techniques
- Illustrate troubleshooting procedures
- Display timing-sensitive operations

11.3 SOP Example: PCB Assembly

SOP-PCB-001: CM4 Installation

Materials Required:

- Validated PCB from Shelf 1
- Programmed CM4 module from Shelf 3
- Anti-static wrist strap

Procedure:

1. Verify PCB serial number against assembly log
2. Connect anti-static wrist strap
3. Remove CM4 from anti-static packaging
4. Align CM4 connector with PCB socket (Image: CM4-alignment.jpg)
5. Press CM4 down until fully seated (Video: CM4-install.mp4)
6. Secure with retention clips
7. Visual verification: No gap between CM4 and PCB

Quality Check:

- CM4 sits flush against PCB surface
- Retention clips properly engaged
- No bent pins or mechanical damage

Expected Time: 2 minutes

11.4 Mistake Analysis Framework

11.4.1 Systematic Error Documentation

Create a mistake log for every production issue:

Date	Issue	Root Cause	Solution	Status
2025-01-15	CM4 boot failure	Wrong image version	Update SOP-SW-001	Closed
2025-01-18	Case fit problem	PCB tolerance stack	Revise mechanical	Open
2025-01-20	Cable disconnect	Insufficient strain relief	Design change	Planning

Tabela 11.1: Production mistake tracking log

11.4.2 Component Availability Issues

Supply chain failure analysis:

Track component obsolescence and supplier issues systematically:

Example: Component unavailability analysis

- **Issue:** RC522 RFID module no longer available from primary supplier
- **Investigation:** Manufacturer discontinued this specific variant
- **Root cause:** Single-source dependency without backup suppliers

- **Solution:** Identify three alternative suppliers, test compatibility
- **Prevention:** Add supplier diversity requirements to BOM management

Supplier performance tracking:

- Delivery time reliability
- Quality consistency
- Communication responsiveness
- Price stability
- Stock availability patterns

11.4.3 Design Optimization Opportunities

Overengineering identification:

Use production data to optimize future designs:

Example: Memory usage analysis

- **Observation:** 4GB RAM modules consistently show 60% unused capacity
- **Analysis:** Application never exceeds 1.5GB under peak load
- **Conclusion:** 2GB modules adequate for application requirements
- **Action:** Switch to 2GB CM4 variant for cost reduction
- **Savings:** €15 per unit cost reduction

Reliability data analysis:

- **Power supply failures:** After 12 months, 8% failure rate

- **Investigation:** Thermal stress in inadequately ventilated enclosures
- **Solution:** Specify higher temperature rating for power components
- **Design change:** Add ventilation requirements to enclosure specification

11.5 Process Improvement Implementation

11.5.1 SOP Version Control

Treat SOPs like software code:

Version control requirements:

- Date and version number on every SOP
- Change log documenting modifications
- Previous version archive for rollback capability
- Author identification and approval signature

SOP update triggers:

- Component substitution requirements
- Assembly time optimization opportunities
- Quality issue resolution
- Tool or equipment changes

11.5.2 Training and Verification

SOP validation process:

1. New operator follows SOP independently
2. Supervisor observes and documents deviations
3. Timing and quality metrics recorded
4. SOP revised based on observed difficulties
5. Re-test with different operator for verification

11.6 Documentation Tools and Infrastructure

11.6.1 Simple Documentation System

Recommended toolchain:

- **Written procedures:** Google Docs or similar collaborative platform
- **Image management:** Standardized naming convention with date stamps
- **Video hosting:** Private YouTube channel or local file server
- **Version control:** Simple folder structure with version numbers

Avoid over-engineering: Complex documentation systems often go unused. Simple, accessible tools encourage consistent updates.

11.6.2 Mobile-Friendly Access

Production workers need mobile access to SOPs:

Mobile requirements:

- Large, clear images visible on phone screens
- Video playback without additional software
- Offline access capability for network-poor environments
- Quick search functionality for specific procedures

11.7 Continuous Improvement Culture

11.7.1 Feedback Integration

Create systematic feedback collection:

Production operator feedback:

- Weekly SOP improvement suggestions
- Assembly time and difficulty reporting
- Quality issue identification
- Tool and equipment optimization requests

Customer feedback integration:

- Field failure analysis and root cause investigation
- Feature request evaluation for design changes
- Installation and setup difficulty reports
- Long-term reliability data collection

11.7.2 Metrics-Driven Improvement

Key documentation metrics:

- SOP compliance rate (percentage of procedures followed correctly)
- Assembly time variance (consistency indicator)
- Rework rate reduction over time
- New operator training time requirements

11.8 Documentation ROI

Proper documentation investment pays dividends:

Immediate benefits:

- Reduced dependence on your personal involvement
- Consistent quality across different operators
- Faster training of new production workers
- Clear accountability for process steps

Long-term benefits:

- Scalable production beyond single-person operations
- Knowledge preservation during personnel changes
- Systematic improvement rather than ad-hoc fixes
- Foundation for quality certifications and audits

Documentation transforms your hardware production from artisanal craft to systematic manufacturing. The investment in creating comprehensive SOPs and mistake analysis systems enables scaling beyond your personal capacity while maintaining quality and reliability.

Remember: every minute spent documenting procedures saves hours of troubleshooting and retraining later. The goal is building a business that can operate successfully without your constant intervention.

12
Repeat

Scaling from your first successful production run is where the real business begins. You've established a repeatable process, validated your market, and proven you can deliver quality hardware consistently. Now comes the strategic decision: what's next?

The process you've developed works equally well for 10, 100, or 1000 devices. The principles remain constant while the scale changes. This chapter covers how to leverage your proven methodology for sustained growth.

12.1 The Foundation is Built

You now have something valuable: a documented, repeatable process for bringing hardware products to market. This isn't just about your current device—it's a systematic capability you can apply to future products.

What you've established:

- Reliable supplier relationships and procurement processes

- Quality assurance procedures that scale with volume
- Software deployment and update mechanisms
- Customer support infrastructure
- Manufacturing cost models and profit margins

12.2 Planning Your Next Device

12.2.1 Leverage Existing Infrastructure

Don't start from scratch. Your next device should build upon the foundation you've created:

Reuse proven components that never failed:

- Same CM4/CM5 platform for consistent software stack
- Established connector types and cable assemblies with zero failure history
- Proven enclosure manufacturing partnerships
- Validated power supply architectures that survived field testing
- RFID modules, sensors, or interfaces with demonstrated reliability

Avoid changing what works: If a component survived 100+ devices in the field without failure, that's valuable validation data. Component substitution introduces risk without benefit.

Reuse proven processes:

- Spider prototype methodology
- PCB design and manufacturing workflow

- Software development and deployment procedures
- Quality assurance and testing protocols that caught issues

> **Evolution vs. Stability Trade-off**
>
> Technology constantly evolves, creating incompatibilities. New CM versions may break existing drivers. Updated OS releases can introduce software incompatibilities. The temptation to upgrade for the sake of upgrading often introduces more problems than benefits.
> Stick with proven technology stacks until compelling customer value justifies the migration risk.

12.2.2 Market-Driven Innovation

Your next device should address customer feedback and market opportunities:

Customer-driven features: Listen to support requests and enhancement suggestions from existing customers. They're telling you exactly what the market needs.

Adjacent market opportunities: If you've built a time attendance system, consider access control, visitor management, or asset tracking applications using similar technology.

12.3 Technology Evolution Management

12.3.1 Raspberry Pi Roadmap Awareness

Stay informed about Raspberry Pi development cycles:

Monitor new releases:

- CM5 adoption timeline and availability

- Software compatibility with new hardware
- Performance improvements vs. cost increases
- Backward compatibility considerations

Migration strategy: Don't chase every new release immediately. Evaluate whether new hardware provides significant customer value before upgrading your proven platform.

> **Technology Transition Risk**
>
> New Raspberry Pi releases often introduce compatibility issues, driver changes, and software stack modifications. Only migrate when the benefits clearly outweigh the stability risks for your specific application.

12.3.2 Component Lifecycle Management

Proactive obsolescence planning:

- Monitor end-of-life announcements for critical components
- Maintain relationships with component suppliers for early notification
- Design flexibility for component substitutions
- Stock strategic components for extended production runs

12.4 Scaling Production Excellence

12.4.1 Volume Progression Strategy

Your proven process scales systematically:

100 to 500 units:

- Refine assembly procedures for efficiency
- Negotiate volume discounts with suppliers
- Consider dedicated assembly workspace
- Implement more sophisticated inventory management

500 to 1000 units:

- Evaluate injection molding for enclosures
- Consider contract manufacturing partnerships
- Implement statistical process control
- Develop formal quality management systems

1000+ units:

- Full contract manufacturing evaluation
- Automated testing and configuration systems
- Supply chain risk management programs
- International market expansion planning

12.5 Customer Success: The Differentiator

12.5.1 After-Sales Excellence

Superior after-sales support differentiates quality hardware companies from competitors. This is where you build customer loyalty and generate referrals.

Proactive support strategies:

- Remote monitoring and health checks
- Predictive maintenance notifications
- Proactive software updates and security patches
- Regular customer check-ins and satisfaction surveys

Response time commitments:

- Acknowledge support requests within 4 hours
- Provide initial diagnosis within 24 hours
- Resolve critical issues within 48 hours
- Maintain 98% customer satisfaction rating

12.5.2 Customer Relationship Management

Long-term customer value:

- Track customer lifetime value, not just initial sale value
- Develop upgrade and expansion opportunities
- Create customer advisory boards for product feedback
- Implement referral and recommendation programs

Support infrastructure scaling:

- Remote diagnostic capabilities built into devices
- Knowledge base and self-service resources
- Escalation procedures for complex technical issues
- Customer success team dedicated to major accounts

12.6 Business Model Evolution

12.6.1 Recurring Revenue Opportunities

Transform one-time hardware sales into ongoing relationships:

Service-based revenue streams:

- Software subscription services
- Remote monitoring and analytics
- Extended warranty and support plans
- Professional services and integration

Platform expansion:

- API access for third-party integrations
- Mobile applications and cloud services
- Data analytics and reporting services
- Integration with enterprise software systems

12.7 Continuous Improvement Culture

12.7.1 Learning Organization

Establish systematic improvement processes:

Regular review cycles:

- Monthly production metrics analysis
- Quarterly customer satisfaction reviews

- Semi-annual technology roadmap updates
- Annual strategic planning and goal setting

Innovation pipeline:

- Allocate 10-15% of resources to next-generation development
- Maintain relationships with research institutions
- Monitor competitor activities and market trends
- Invest in employee training and skill development

12.8 Risk Management and Resilience

12.8.1 Business Continuity Planning

Supply chain resilience:

- Multiple suppliers for critical components
- Geographic diversification of manufacturing
- Strategic inventory buffers for supply disruptions
- Alternative component qualification processes

Technology risk mitigation:

- Avoid single-source technology dependencies
- Maintain backwards compatibility for customer bases
- Regular security updates and vulnerability management
- Disaster recovery and business continuity plans

12.9 The Repeatable Success Formula

You've proven that systematic hardware development works. The formula is:

1. Systematic problem analysis and component selection
2. Methodical prototype development and validation
3. Professional software development with production considerations
4. Documented assembly and quality processes
5. Scalable manufacturing and supply chain management
6. Exceptional customer support and continuous improvement

This process has taken you from idea to 100+ devices in production. The same methodology will take you to 1000+ devices and beyond.

Success indicators for your next device:

- Development timeline 60% shorter than first device
- Lower prototype costs due to reused components and processes
- Faster market validation through existing customer relationships
- Higher profit margins from established supplier relationships
- Reduced risk through proven methodology and infrastructure

The difference between a successful hardware project and a sustainable hardware business is the ability to repeat success systematically. You now have that capability.

12.10 Looking Forward

Your first successful device is the foundation, not the destination. The real opportunity lies in building a portfolio of products that serve related market needs using your proven development and manufacturing capabilities.

Focus on customer success, maintain technology awareness, and apply your systematic approach to new opportunities. The process works—now make it work repeatedly.

Appendix: Essential Resources

This appendix contains resources from my personal experience building and shipping thousands of hardware devices. These are my actual partners and suppliers—companies I've worked with directly and can recommend based on real production scenarios, not theoretical evaluations.

Every entry in this list has been tested through multiple projects and production runs. These relationships were built over years of trial and error, successful deliveries, and occasional failures that taught valuable lessons.

12.11 Component Sourcing

Digi-Key (https://www.digikey.com) Industry standard for electronic components. Excellent search functionality, reliable stock information, and fast shipping. Use for prototyping and small production runs.

Mouser Electronics (https://www.mouser.com) Similar to Digi-Key with slightly different inventory. Good for cross-referencing part availability and pricing.

Farnell (https://www.farnell.com) Major global distributor with strong presence in Europe and Asia. Reliable source for Raspberry Pi products and industrial components. Good for production volumes with competitive pricing.

TME (https://www.tme.eu) European distributor with competitive pricing and good local support in Poland. Useful for cost optimization in European markets.

Botland (https://botland.store) Polish distributor specializing in development boards and maker-friendly components. Good for Raspberry Pi accessories and sensors.

Waveshare (https://www.waveshare.com) Direct manufacturer of Raspberry Pi accessories and industrial modules. Quality varies, but pricing is competitive for development boards and displays.

12.12 Manufacturing Partners

12.12.1 PCB Manufacturing

JLCPCB (https://jlcpcb.com) Exceptional value for PCB manufacturing and assembly. Their SMT assembly service can populate basic components for prototypes. Critical for rapid iteration during development.

LCSC Custom Cables (https://www.lcsc.com/customcables) Outstanding custom cable manufacturing. Clean documentation, reasonable pricing, and reliable quality. Essential for professional-looking prototypes and production units.

12.12.2 Mechanical Manufacturing

Fullbax Formy (https://fullbax-formy.pl/en/) Premier injection molding partner with established China manufacturing relationships. Use for production volumes above 1000 units where custom enclosures are required.

Cubic Inch (https://cubicinch.pl/en/home/) Leading MJF (Multi Jet Fusion) 3D printing service. Superior surface finish and mechanical properties compared to FDM printing. Ideal for functional prototypes and low-volume production parts.

Kradex (https://www.kradex.com.pl/?lang=en) Extensive catalog of ready-made enclosures. Avoid custom tooling costs by designing your PCB to fit standard enclosures. Significant cost savings for smaller production runs.

12.13 Raspberry Pi Compute Module Solutions

CM4/CM5 Production Base Board (https://shop.razniewski.eu/p/cm4pb) Custom base board designed for production use with integrated RFID, RTC, and standard interfaces. Eliminates need for custom carrier board development in many applications.

CM4/CM5 Programmer (https://shop.razniewski.eu/p/cm4prog) Essential tool for Compute Module development. Enables reliable flashing and recovery of CM4/CM5 modules during development and production.

12.14 Cloud Infrastructure

Hetzner (https://www.hetzner.com) European cloud provider with excellent price-to-performance ratio. Particularly strong for applications requiring GDPR compliance and European data residency.

Balena Cloud (https://www.balena.io/cloud) Specialized IoT device management platform. Provides over-the-air updates, remote access, and fleet management capabilities. Consider for projects requiring remote device management.

12.15 Software Development

Pi-Gen (https://github.com/RPi-Distro/pi-gen) Official Raspberry Pi OS build system. Essential for creating custom, reproducible

OS images for production devices. Steep learning curve but provides complete control over the software stack.

12.16 Evaluation Criteria

When selecting suppliers and partners, prioritize these factors:

1. **Reliability:** Consistent delivery times and quality standards
2. **Communication:** Responsive technical support and clear documentation
3. **Scalability:** Ability to handle growth from prototype to production volumes
4. **Geographic proximity:** Shorter supply chains reduce risk and shipping costs
5. **Technical capabilities:** Understanding of your specific requirements and constraints

12.17 Cost Optimization Strategy

Development Phase: Use premium suppliers (Digi-Key, Mouser) for fast iteration and reliable components.

Pre-production: Evaluate cost alternatives (TME, direct manufacturers) while maintaining quality standards.

Production: Establish relationships with multiple suppliers to ensure continuity and competitive pricing.

12.18 Warning: Supplier Risks

Critical Supplier Considerations

Single-source dependencies: Never rely on a single supplier for critical components, especially for production volumes.
Quality variability: Lower-cost suppliers may have inconsistent quality. Always order samples before committing to large quantities.
Lead time volatility: Global supply chain disruptions can extend lead times from weeks to months. Plan accordingly.
Minimum order quantities: Production suppliers often require larger minimum orders than development-phase suppliers.

Remember: These resources represent years of trial and error. Each has been validated in real production scenarios, but your specific requirements may lead to different optimal choices. Use this as a starting point, not a definitive solution.

From prototype to 100+ commercial devices in production

This systematic guide provides frameworks for building hardware businesses with Raspberry Pi. Based on real experience from shipping over 5,000 devices worldwide.

Learn the systematic approach to:

- Analyze problems and select components methodically
- Build "spider"prototypes that validate concepts
- Design for automated PCB assembly (no manual soldering)
- Scale manufacturing from 5 to 100+ units
- Plan production-ready software architecture
- Navigate certification and supplier relationships

For engineers and entrepreneurs ready to move beyond hobby projects.

RAZ PUBLISH

ADAM RAŹNIEWSKI

www.ingramcontent.com/pod-product-compliance
Lightning Source LLC
Chambersburg PA
CBHW050528240926
51846CB00003B/738
* 9 7 8 8 3 9 7 7 3 9 6 2 8 *